The Problem With Unicorns

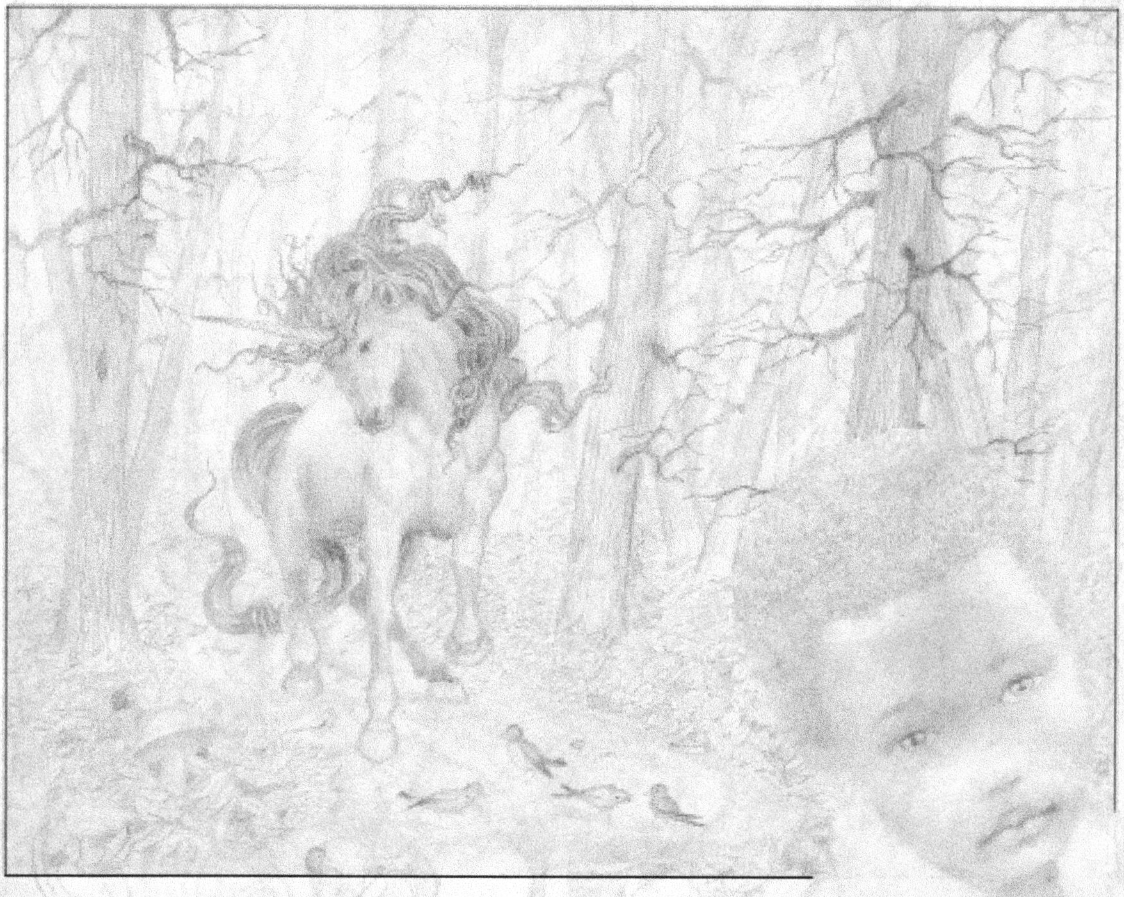

Written and Illustrated
by
Storm Talifero

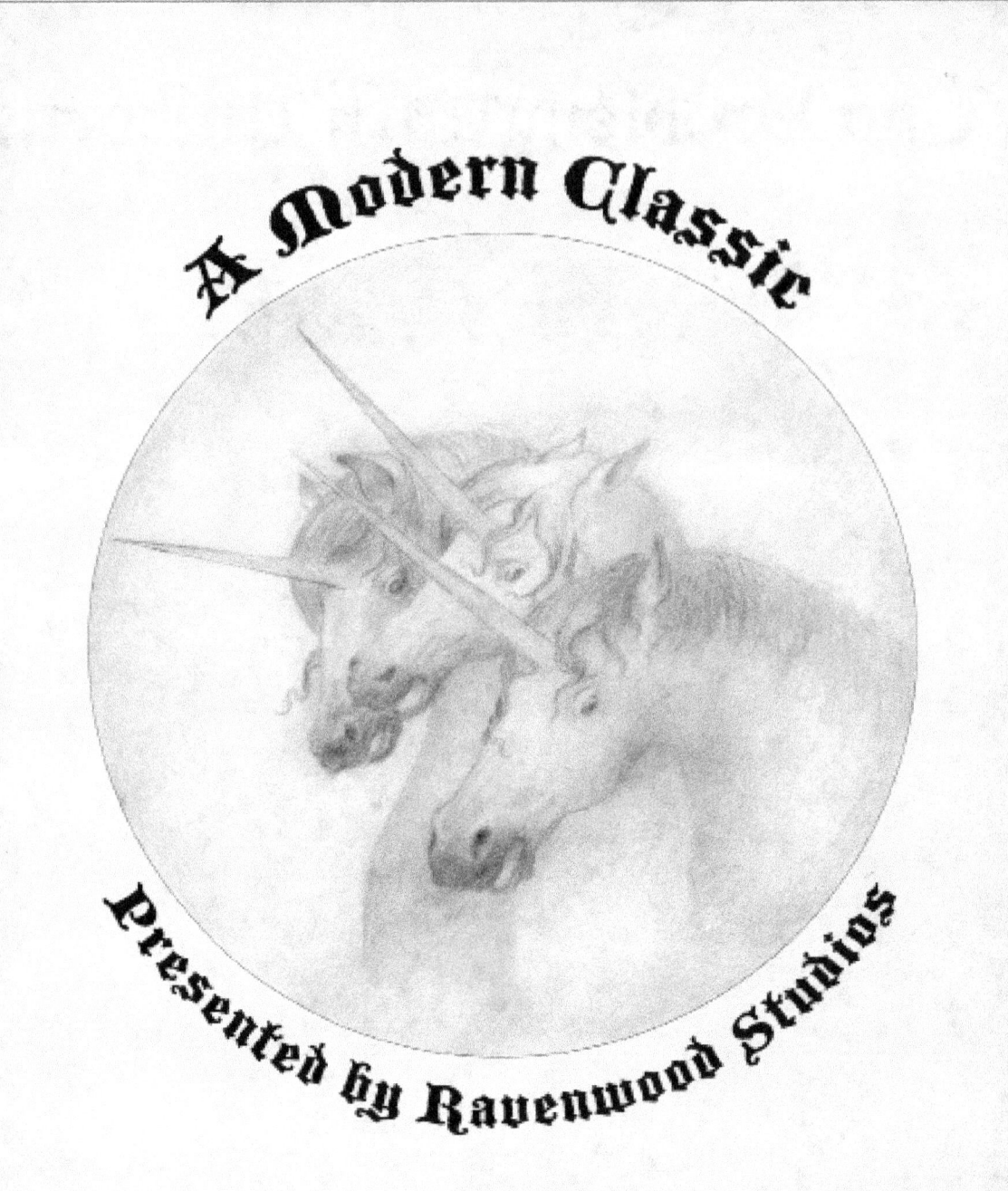

A Modern Classic

Presented by Ravenwood Studios

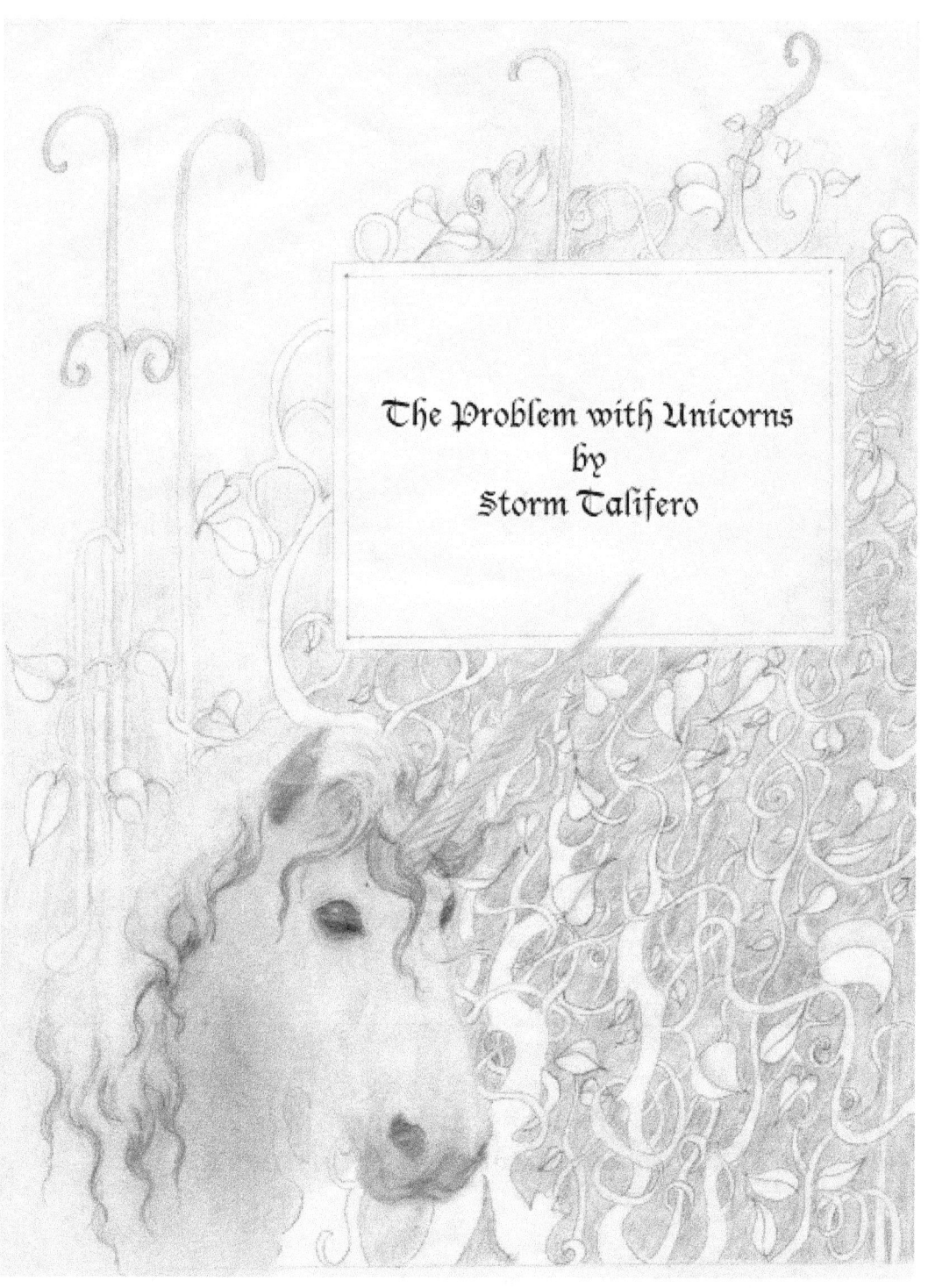

The Problem with Unicorns
by
Storm Talifero

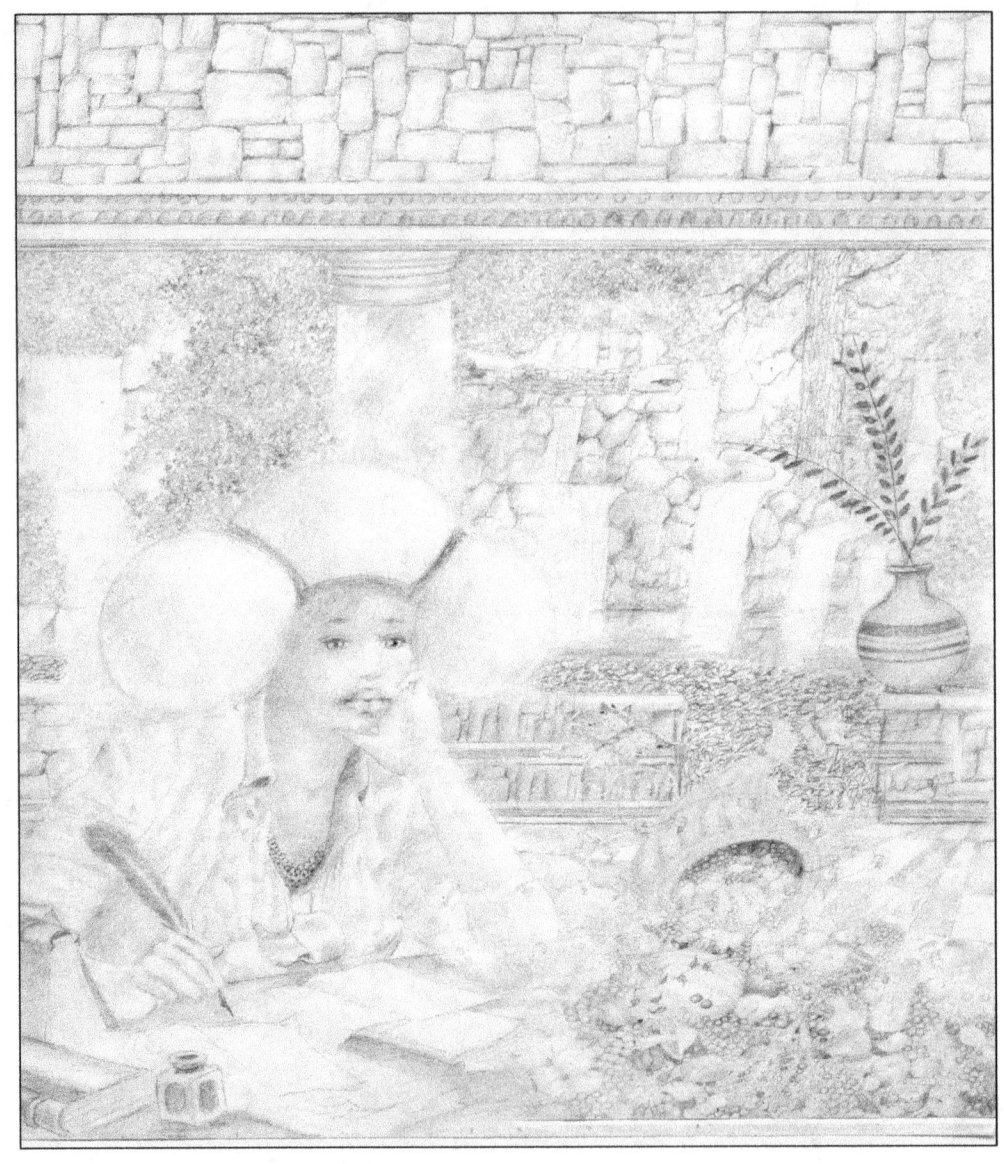

**The Princess in her palace
Dreams of music on the breeze**

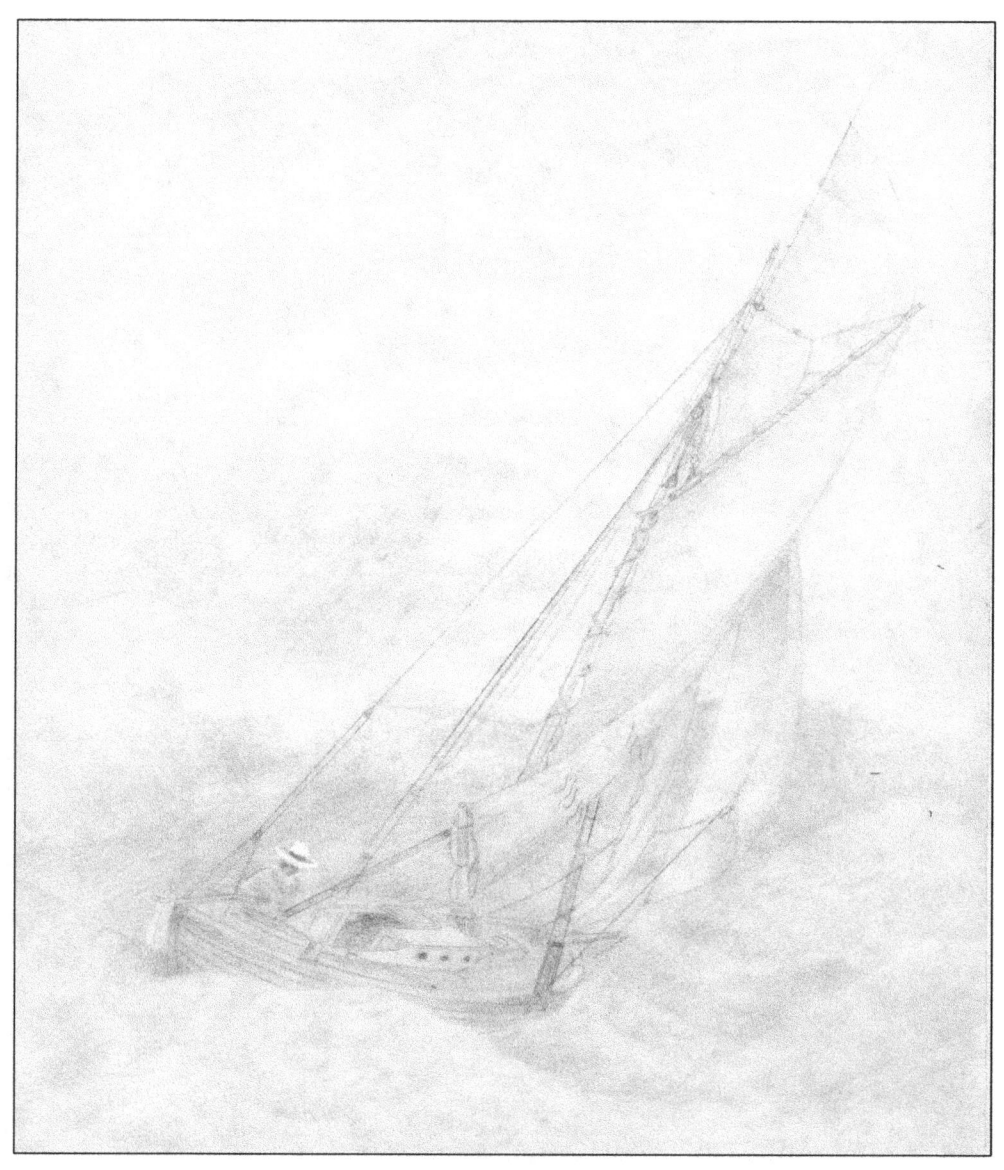

Then comes a wandering minstrel
From across the stormy seas

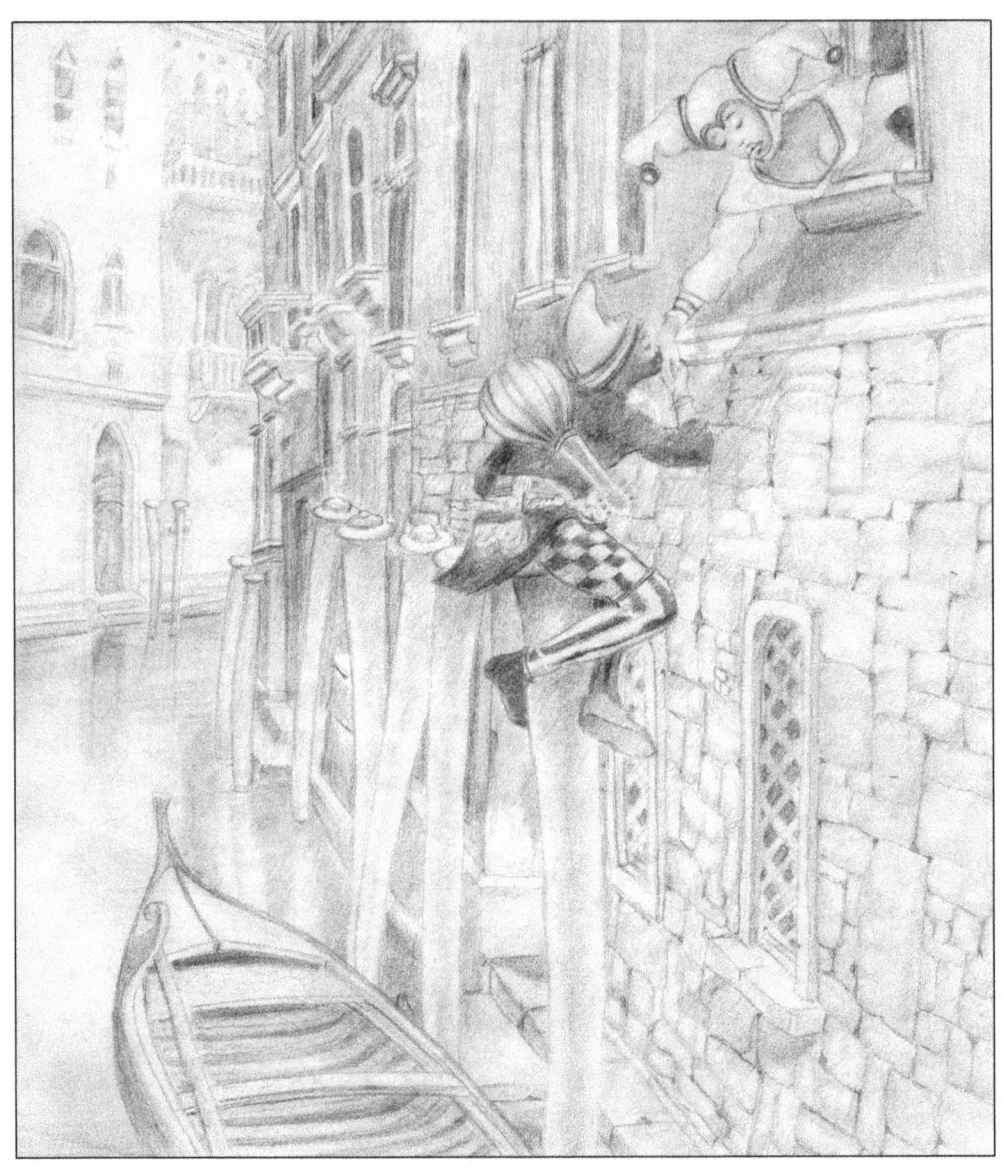

Like voices in the distance
Reflections on the water

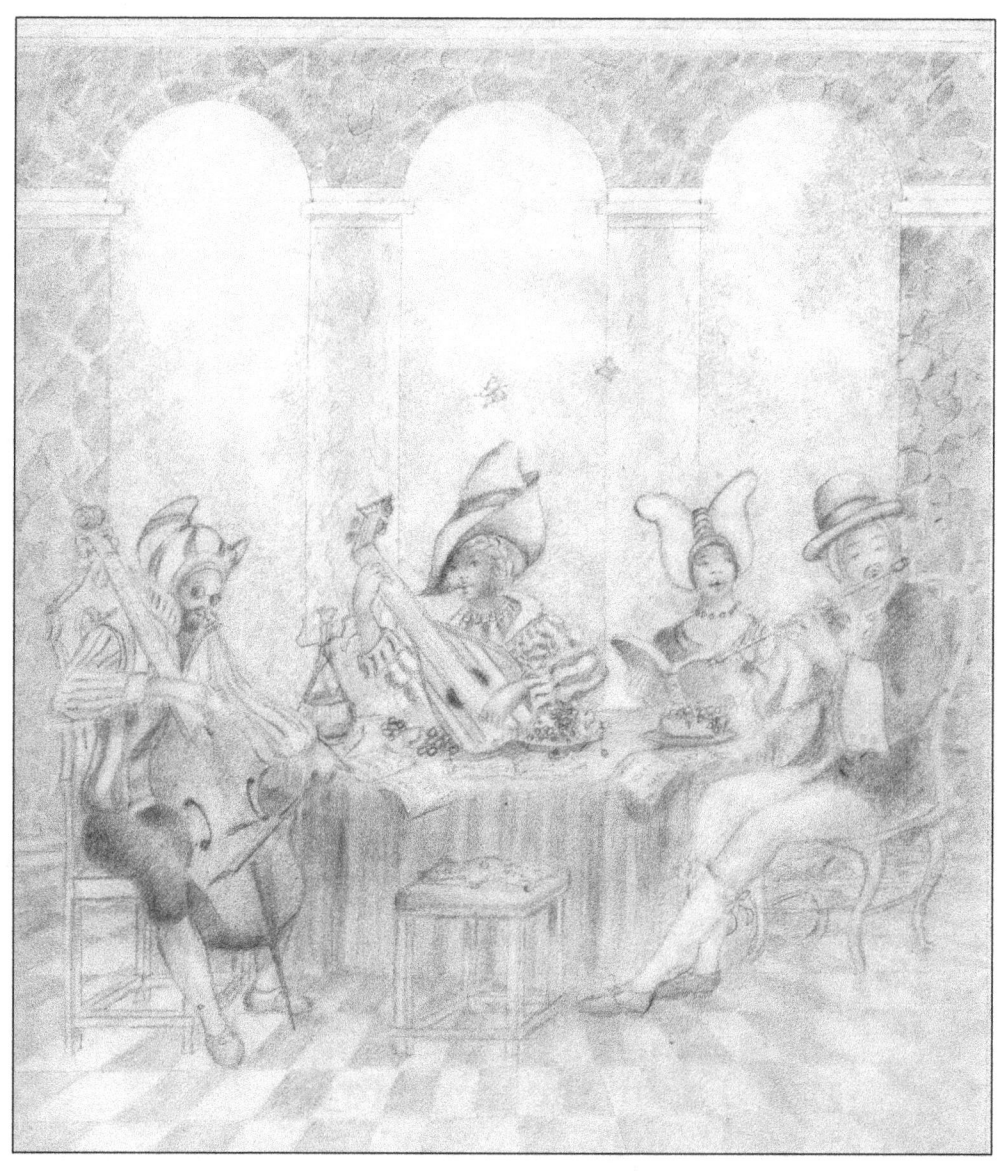

The minstrel spins his stories
For the king's lovely daughter

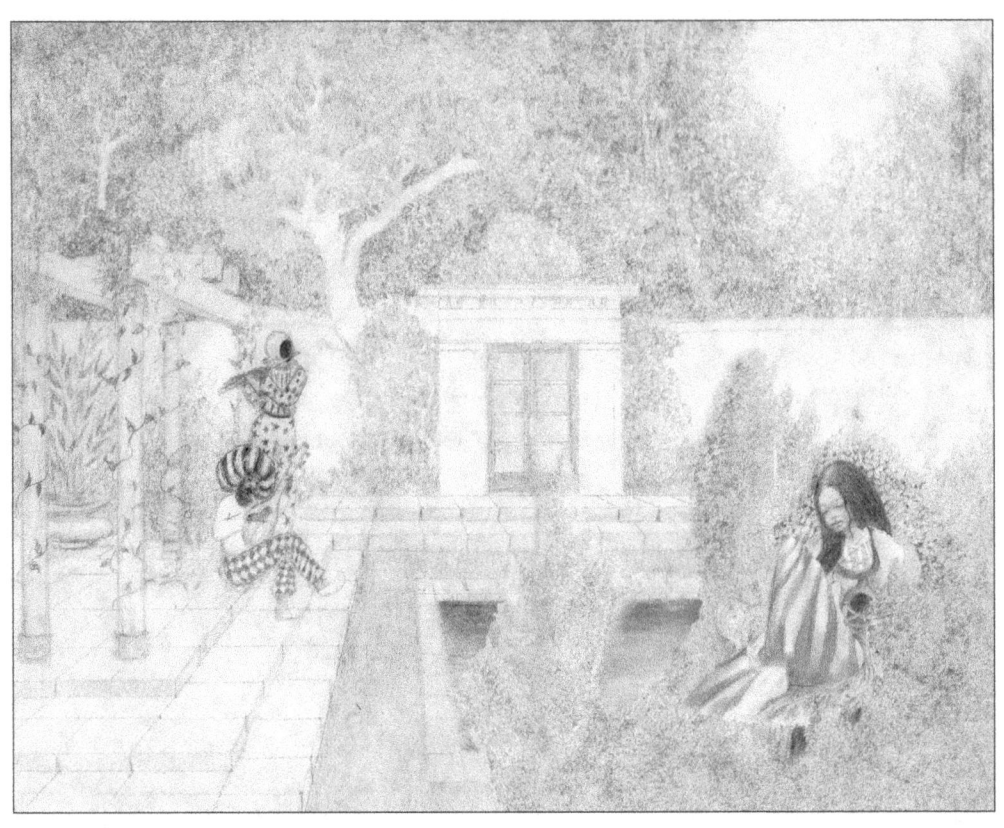

For she's a king's daughter
For all the world to see
Ethereal her loviness
And sweet her vanity

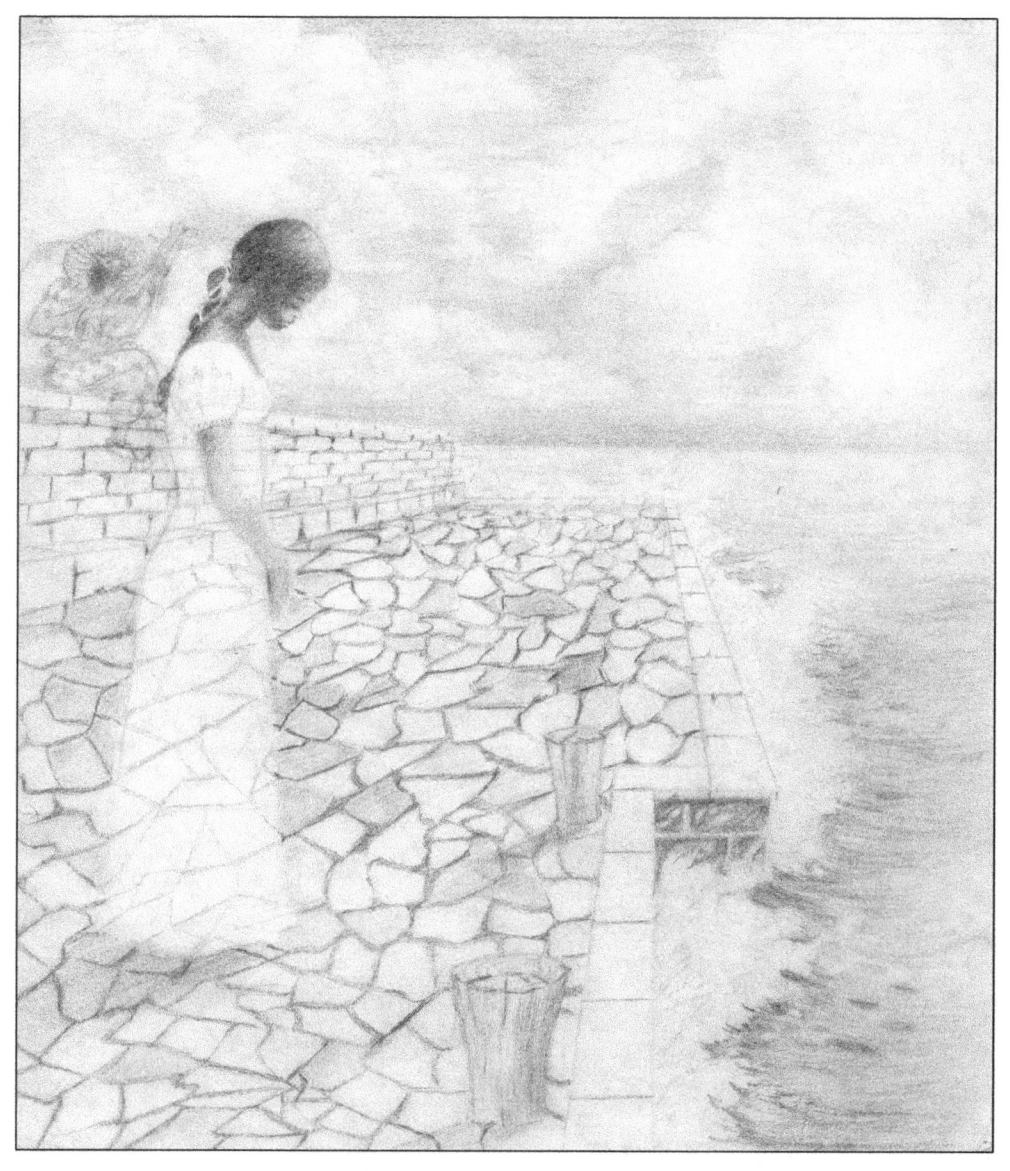

But would she dare to run away
And beg from door to door
For the bliss of the minstrel's kiss
Down by the stony shore

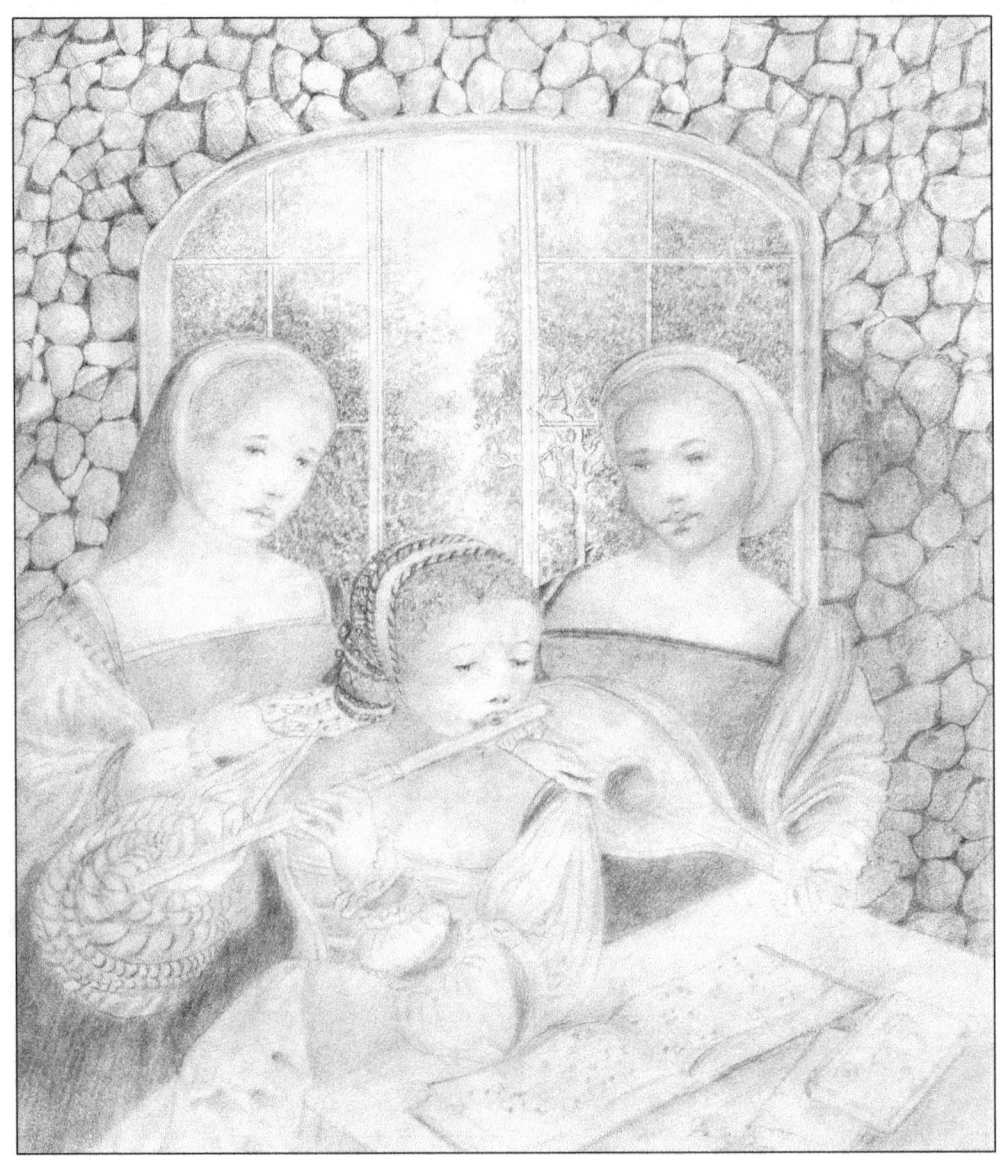

**Her hand-maidens warn her
As you're lovely so be wise**

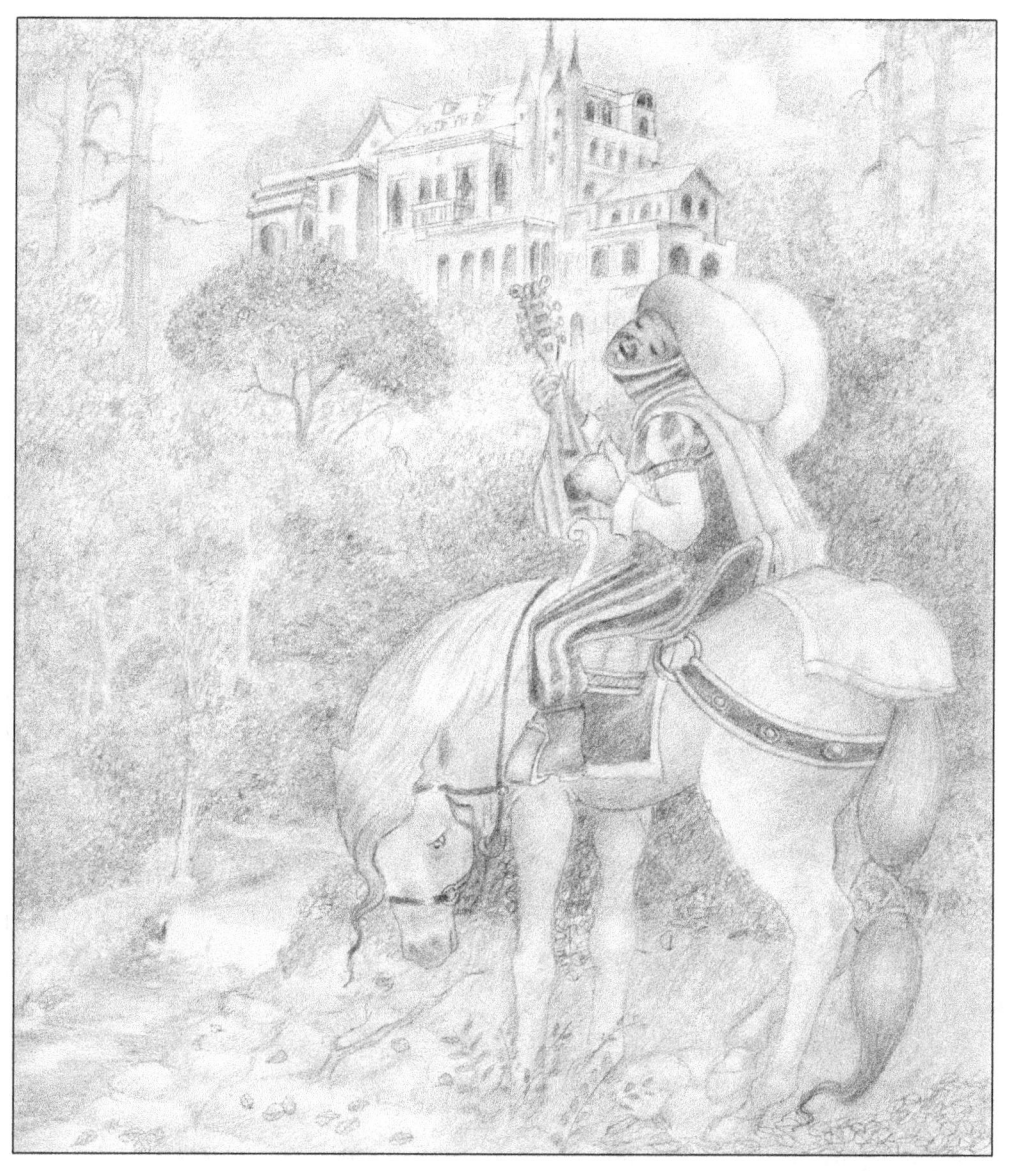

If you desire serenity
Gaze not into his eyes

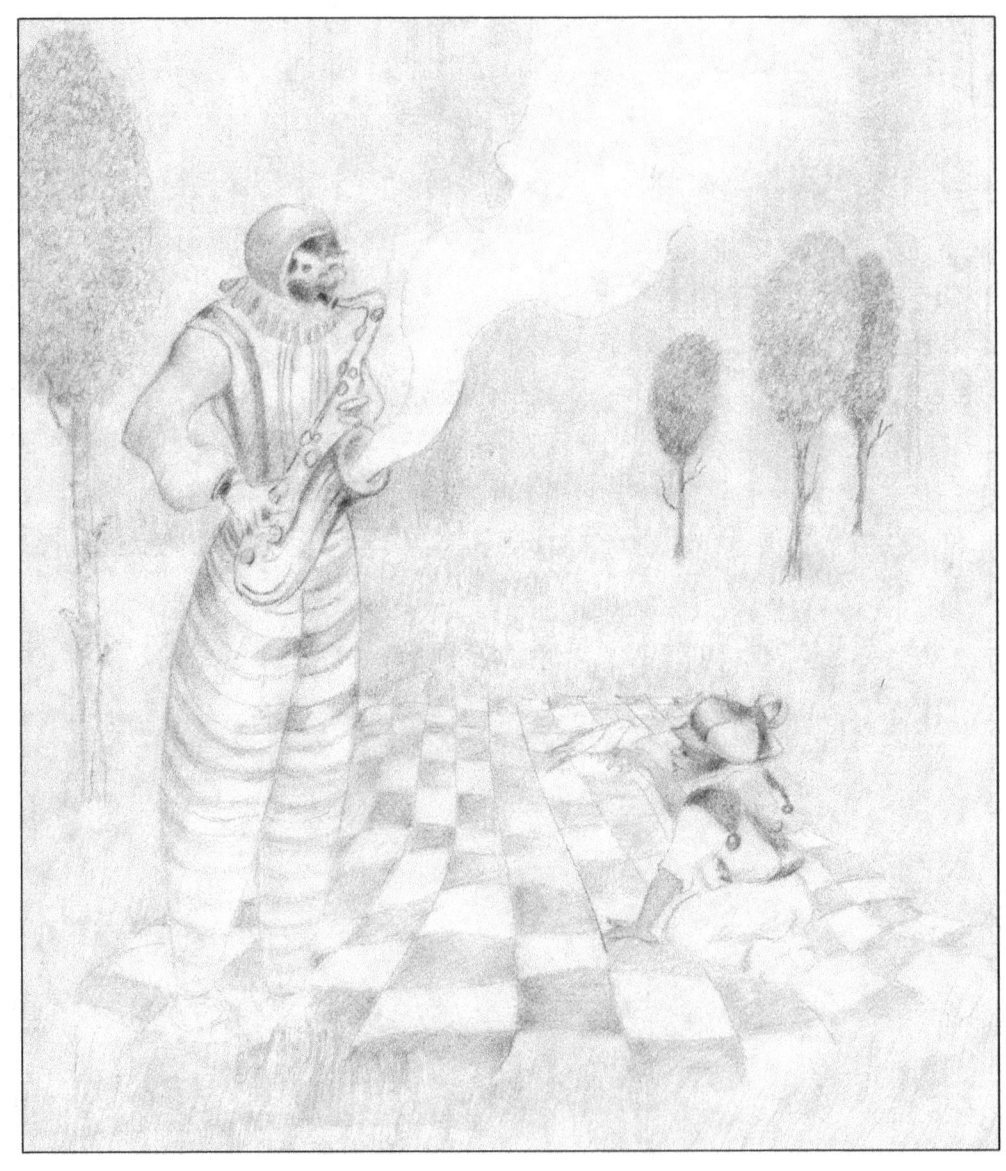

Though he's just a wandering minstrel
If she could have her way

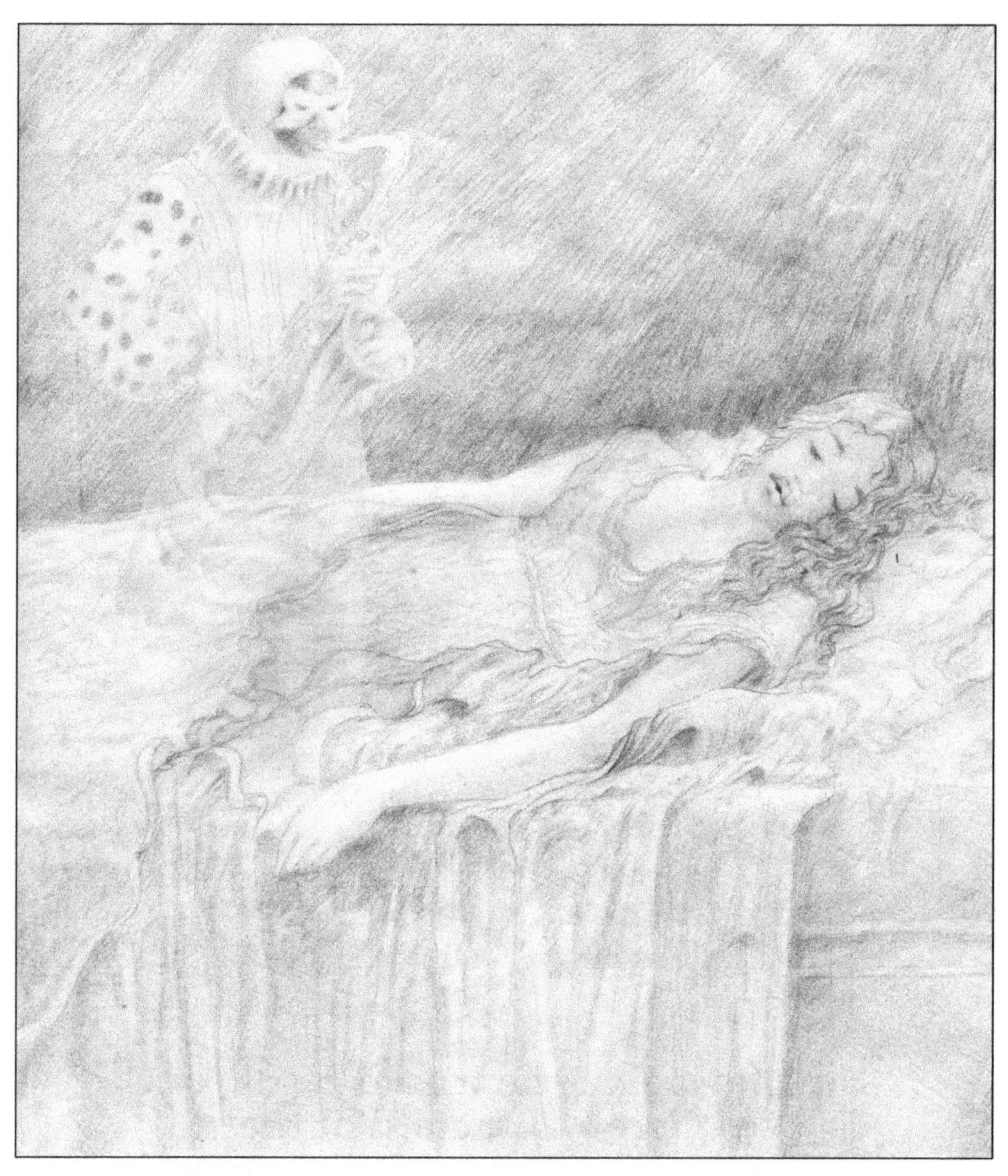

He would be the one she'd choose
Forever and a day

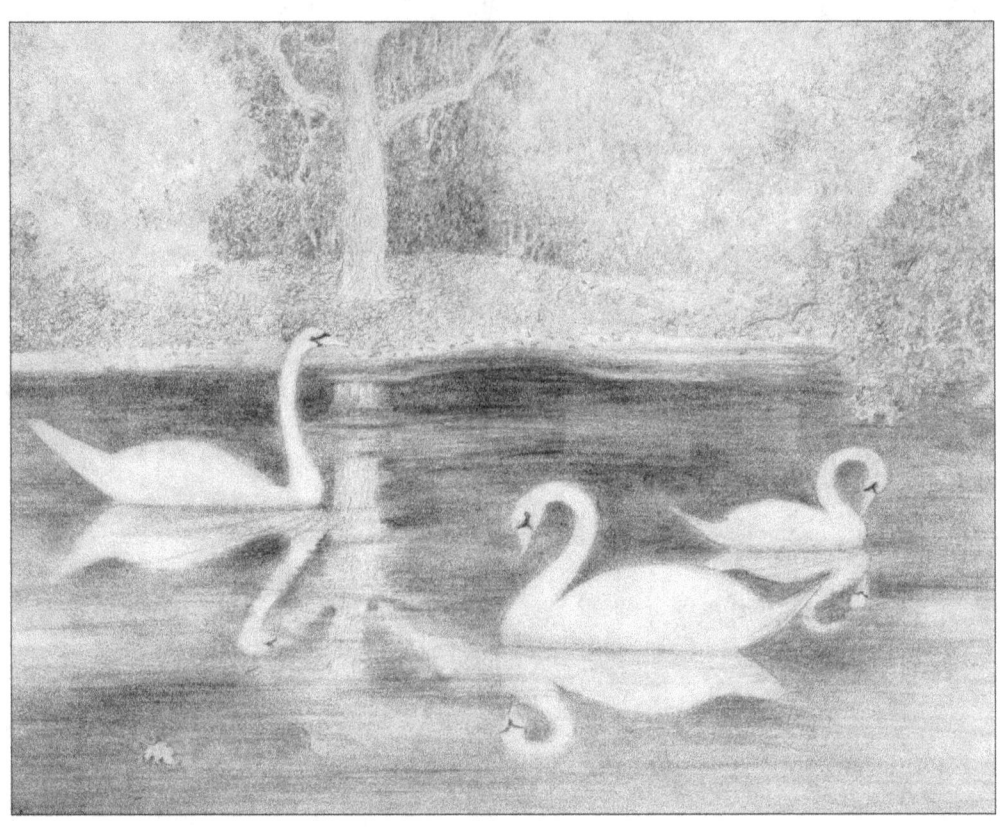

He knows that she would be the one
If ever there was a child of the sun
Tell the king I love his daughter
For she is deep like tranquil water

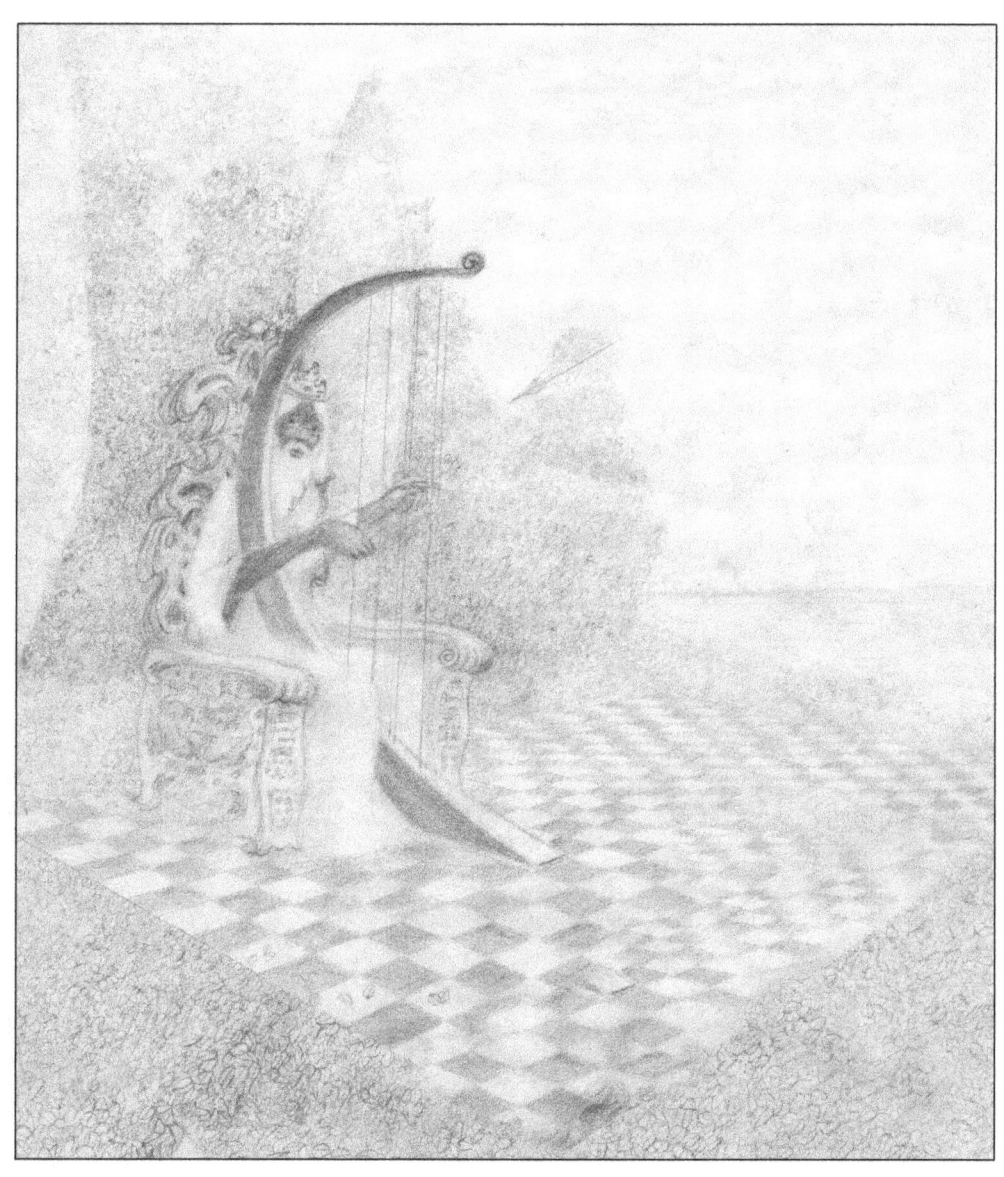

The king is in vexation
This is more than he can stand
The wandering minstrel is in love
And seeks the princess' hand

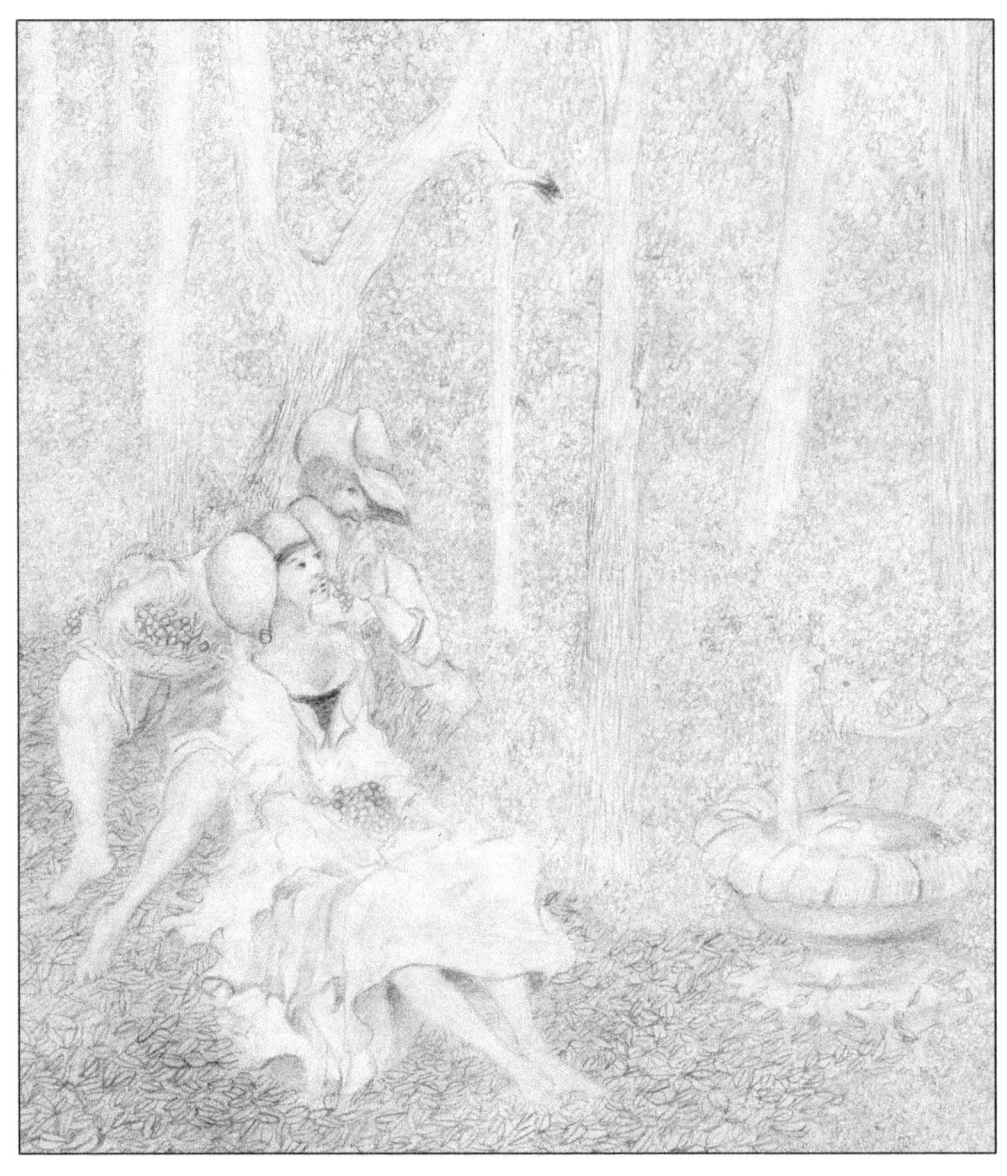

To love the king cannot say no
Nor yet can he say yes

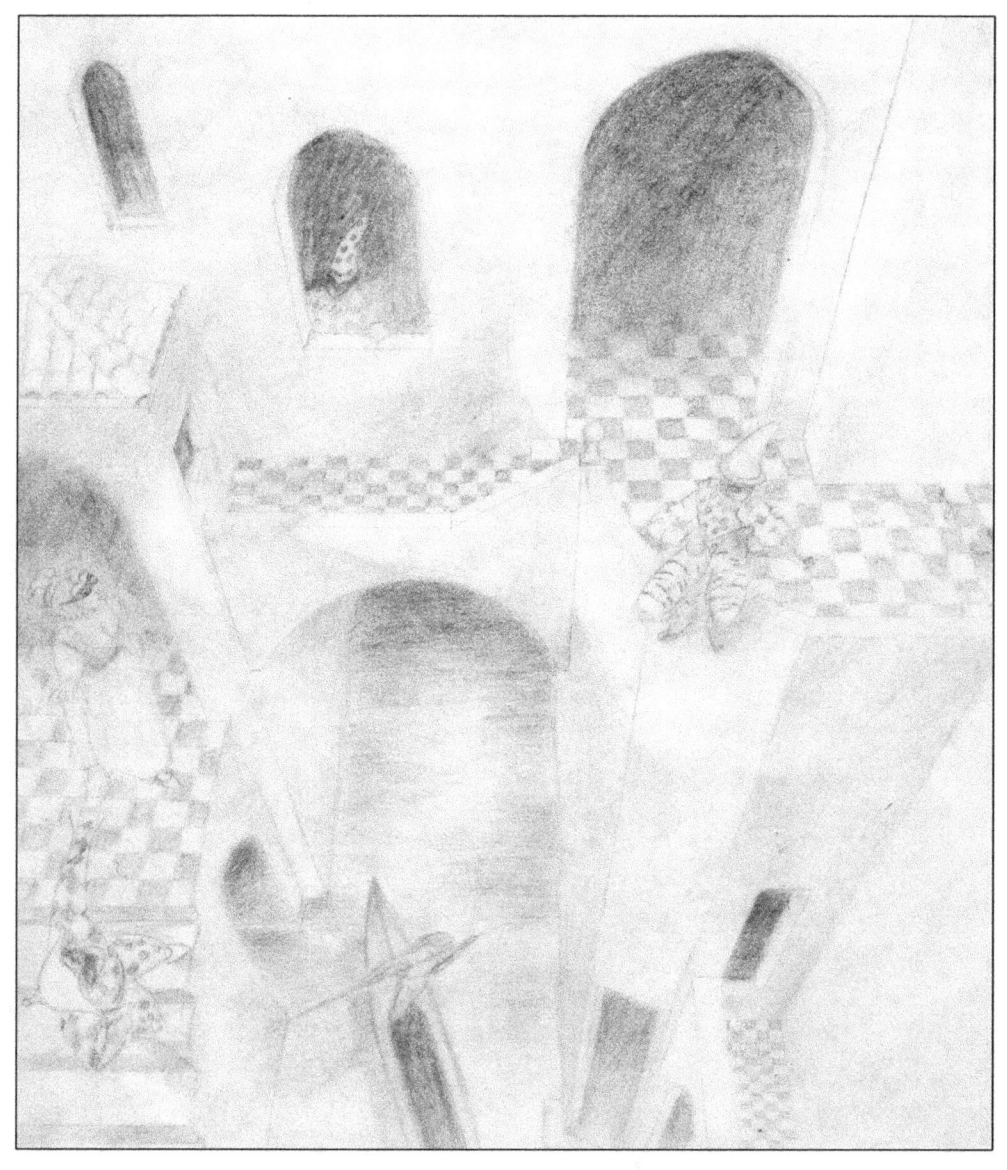

The only thing for him to do
Is send the minstrel on a quest

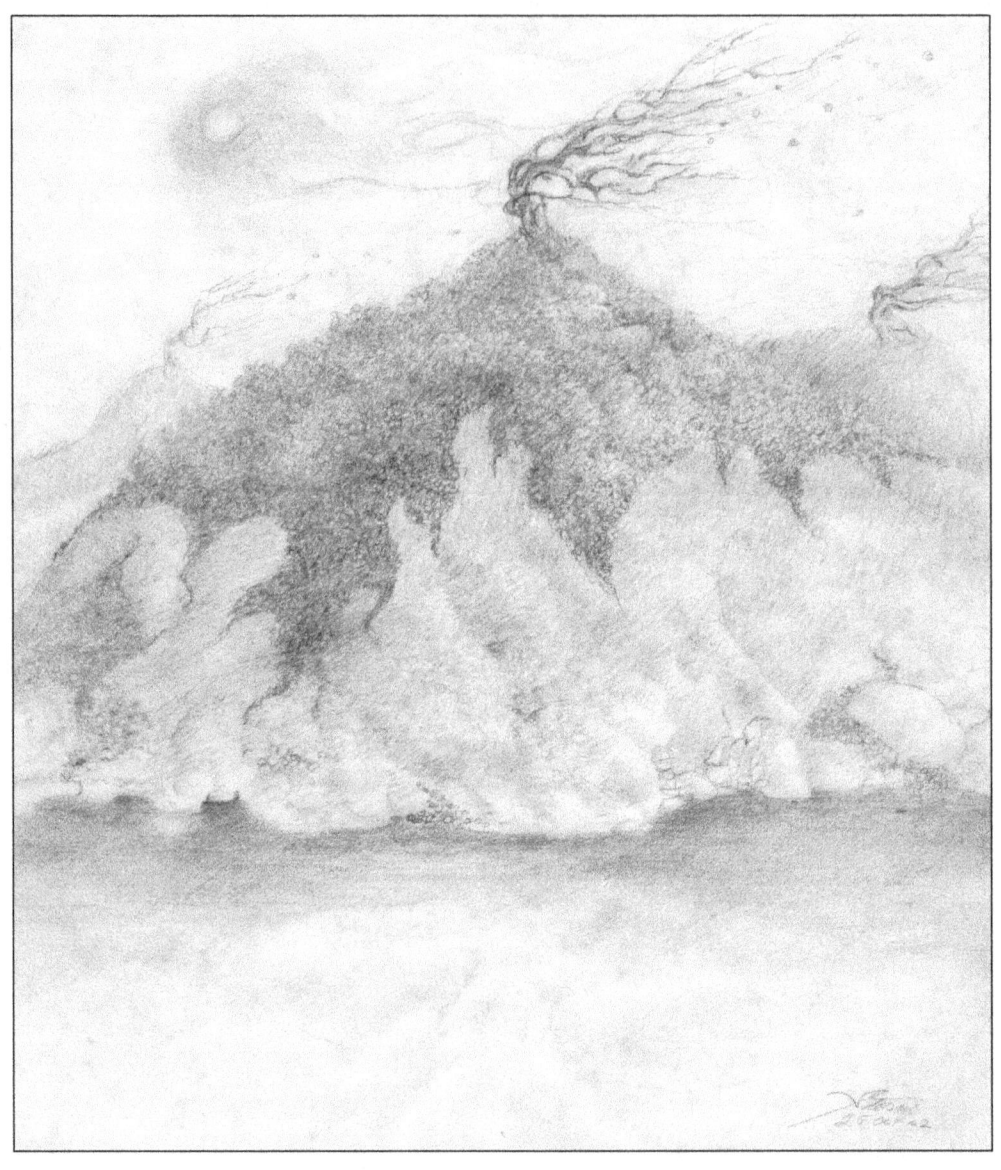

**The king he tells the minstrel
Of an island waterworn**

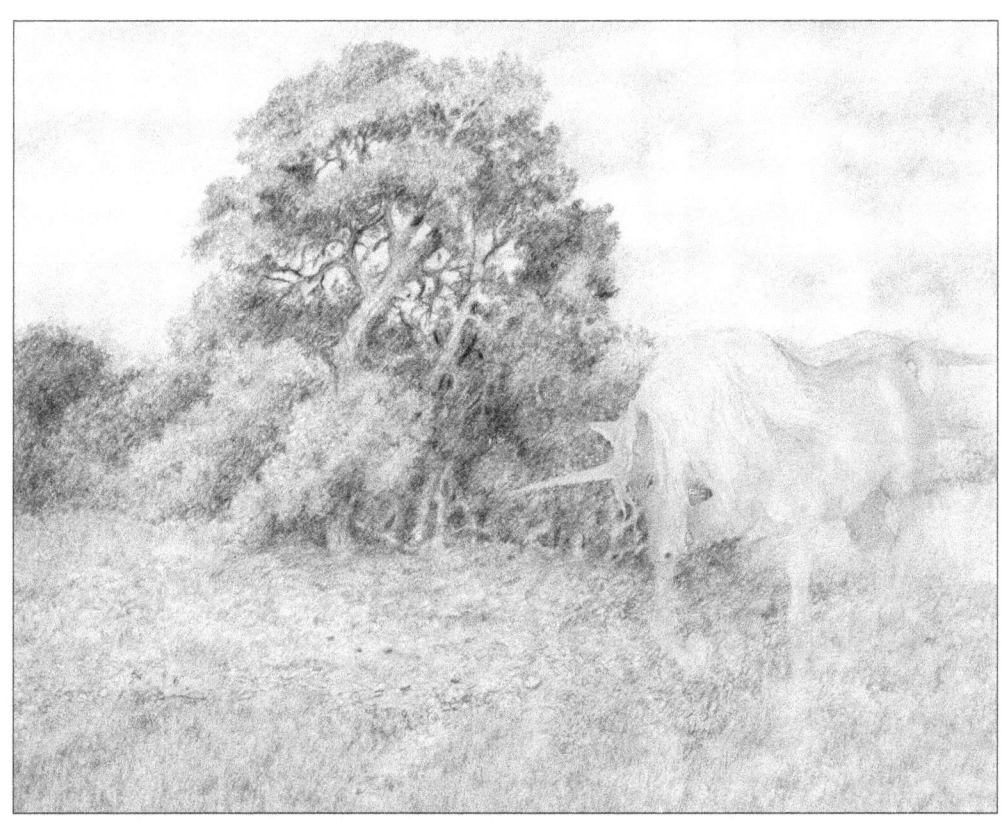

**Where lives in an enchanted wood
The mystic unicorn**

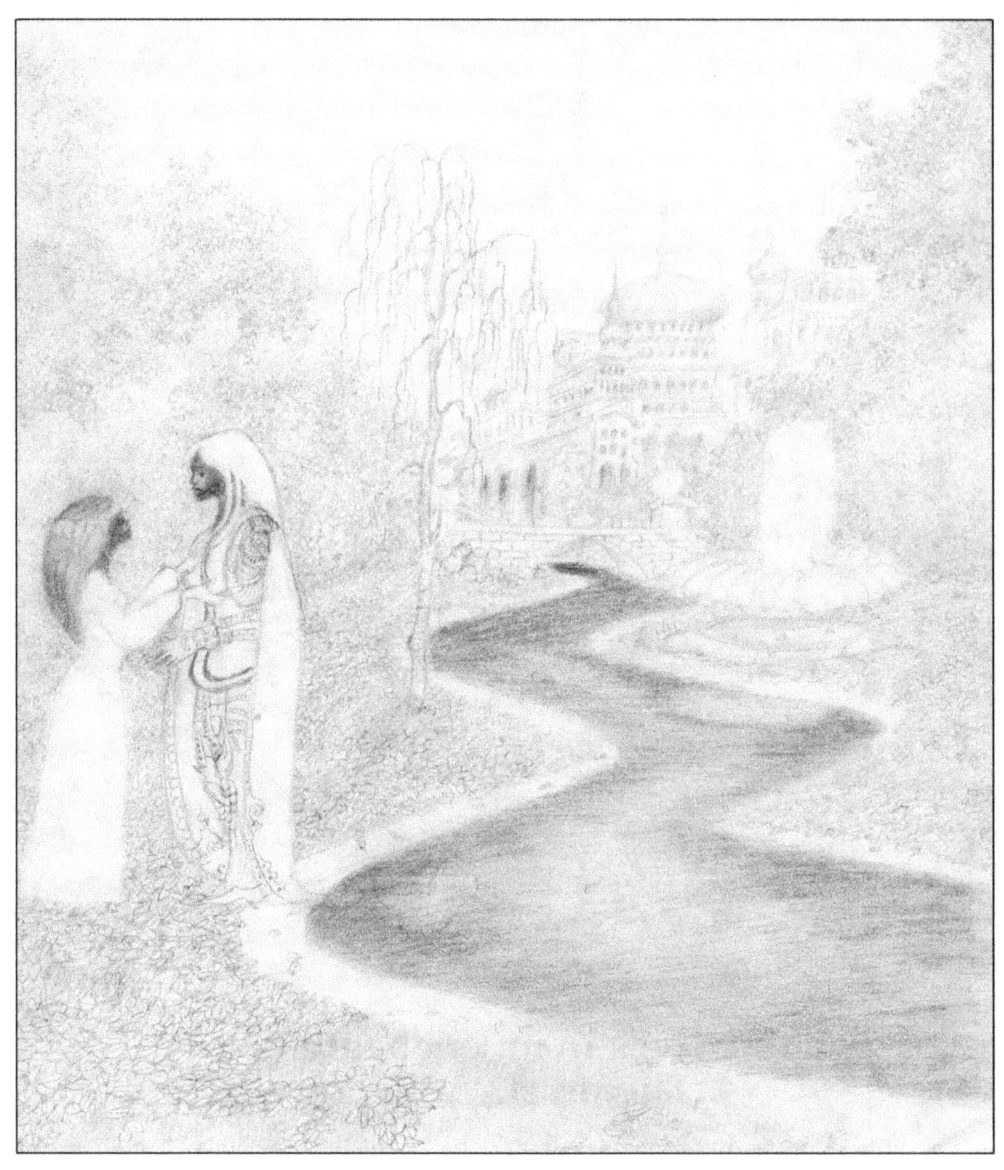

**And if requesting that to you
The princess I shall give**

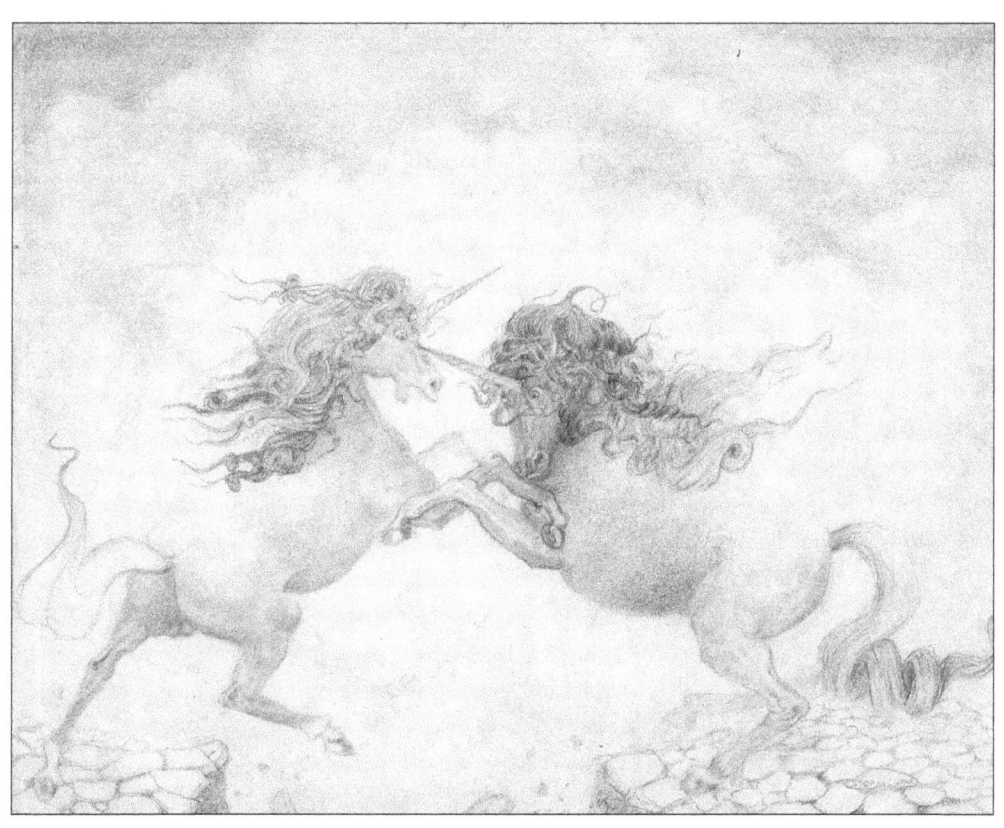

**Then you must find the unicorns
To prove that they still live**

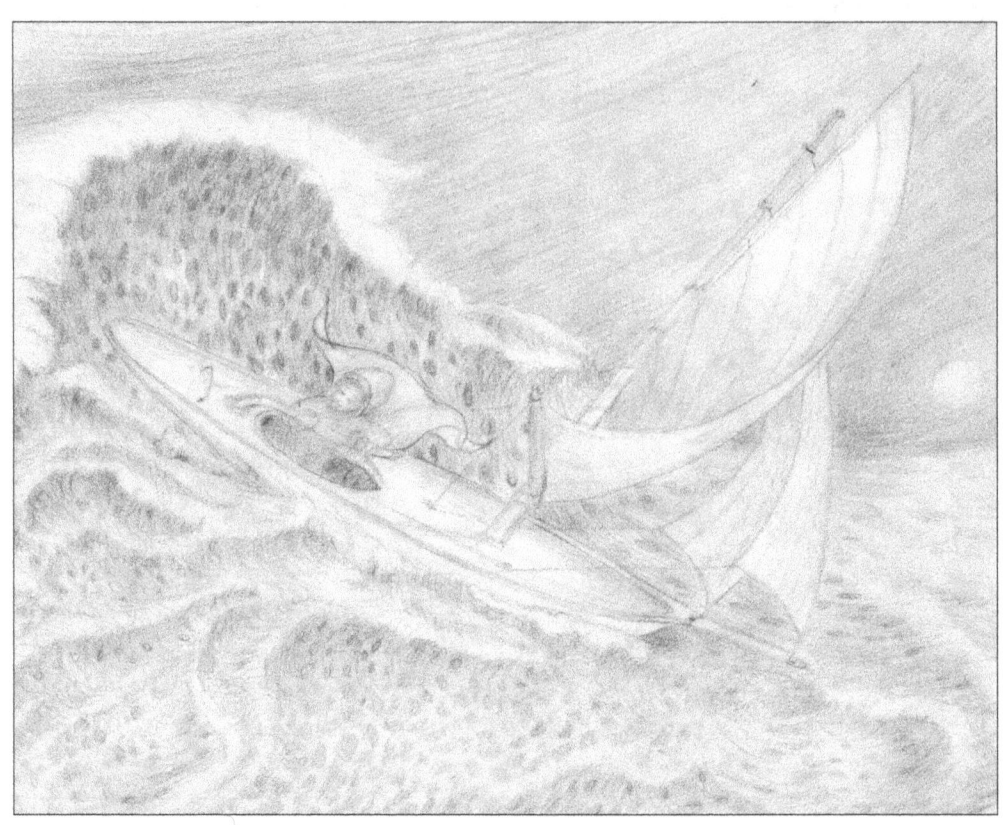

On a dark and savage sea
The minstrel's boat is tossed

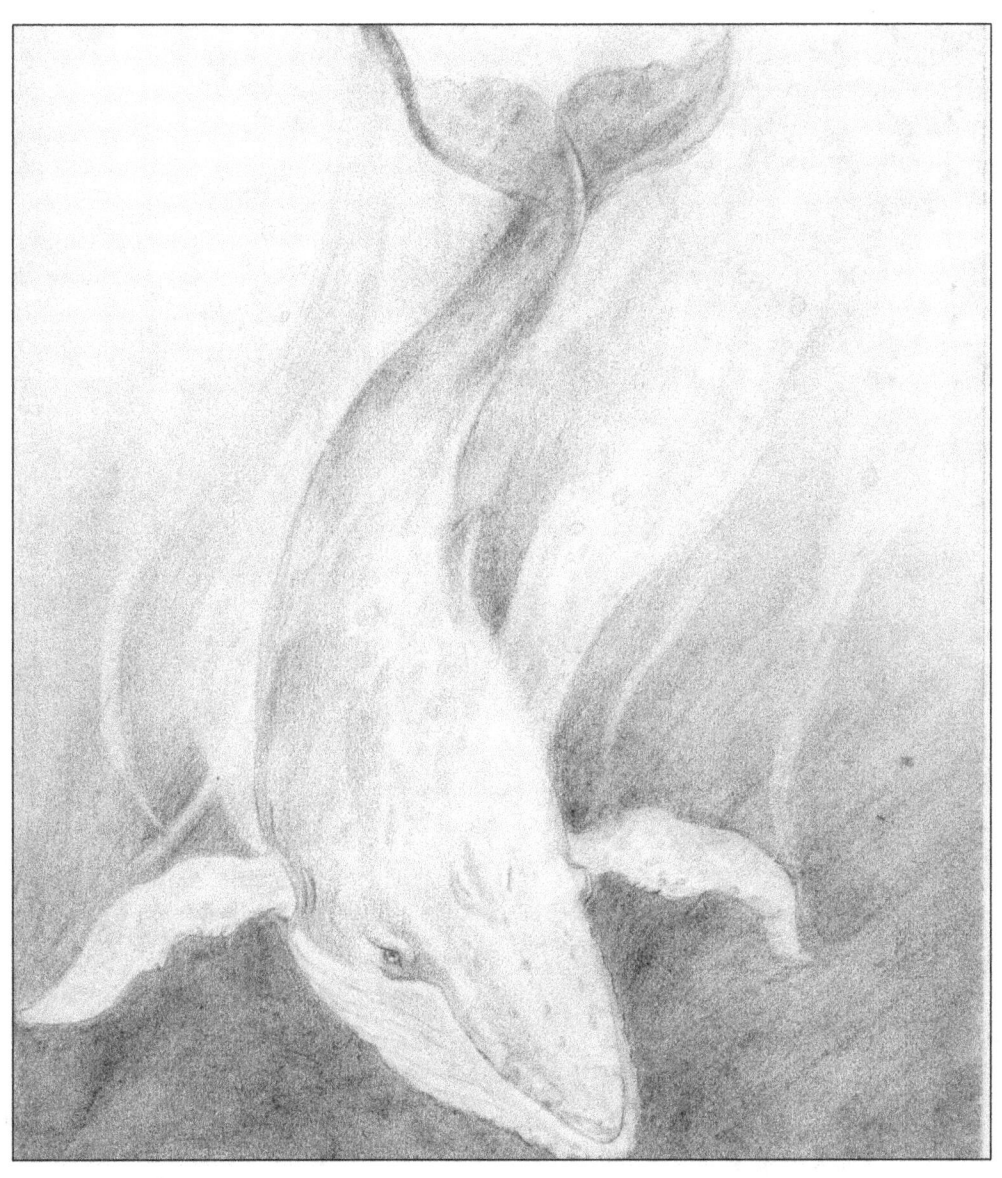

His sails luff, his compass spins
There is no doubt he's lost

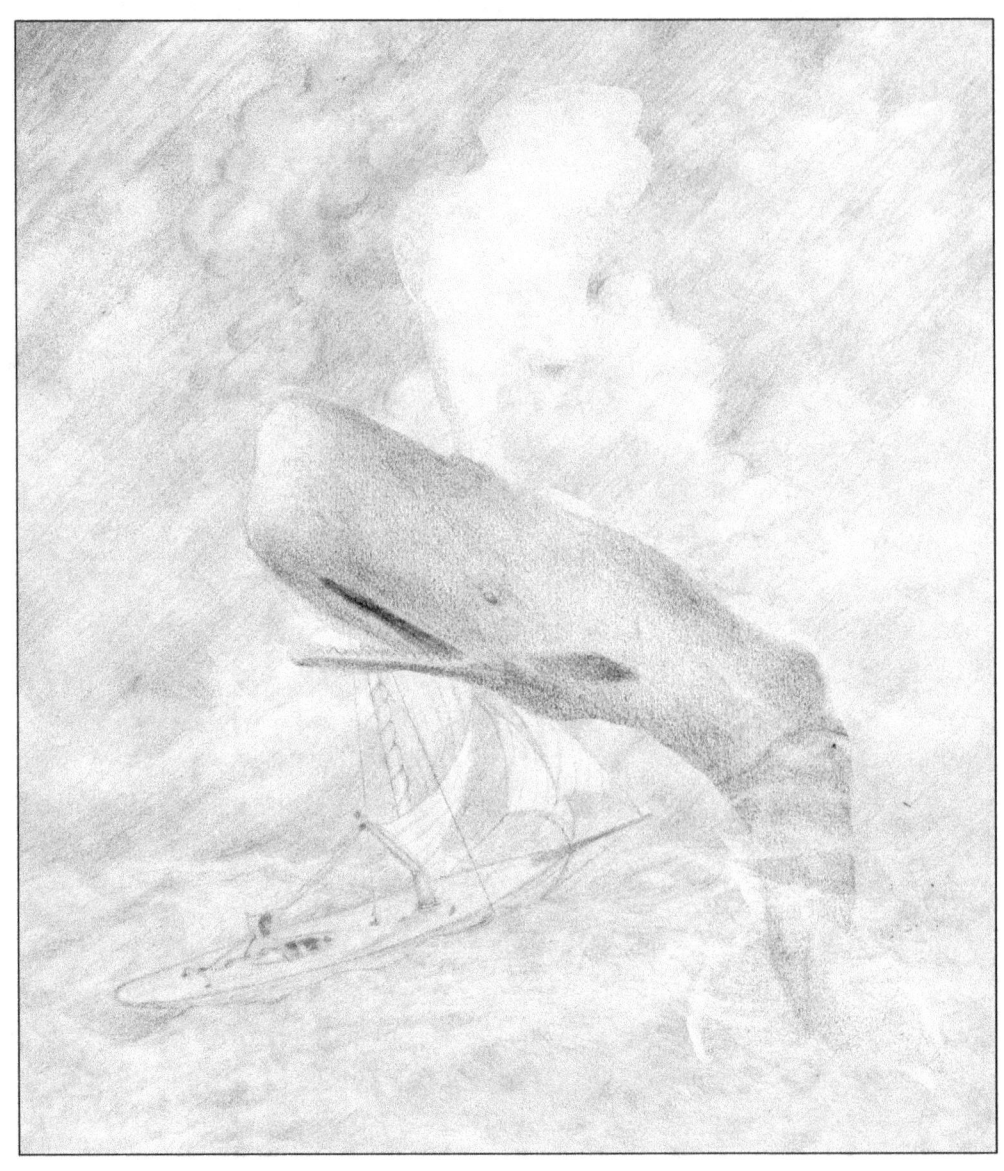

A monstrous whale rises up
Breaching the cruel seas

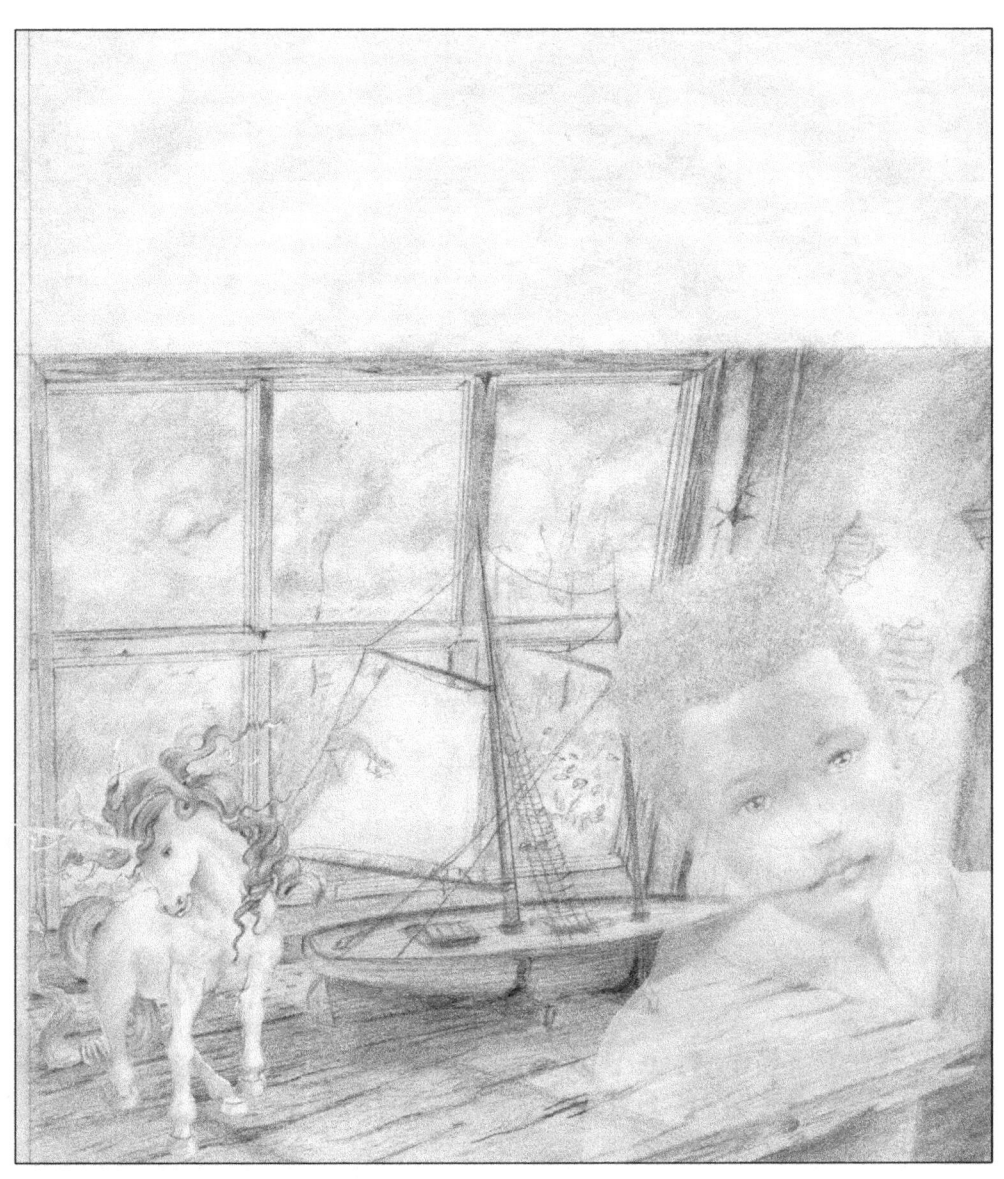

The minstrel views at once his life
Flash by in memories

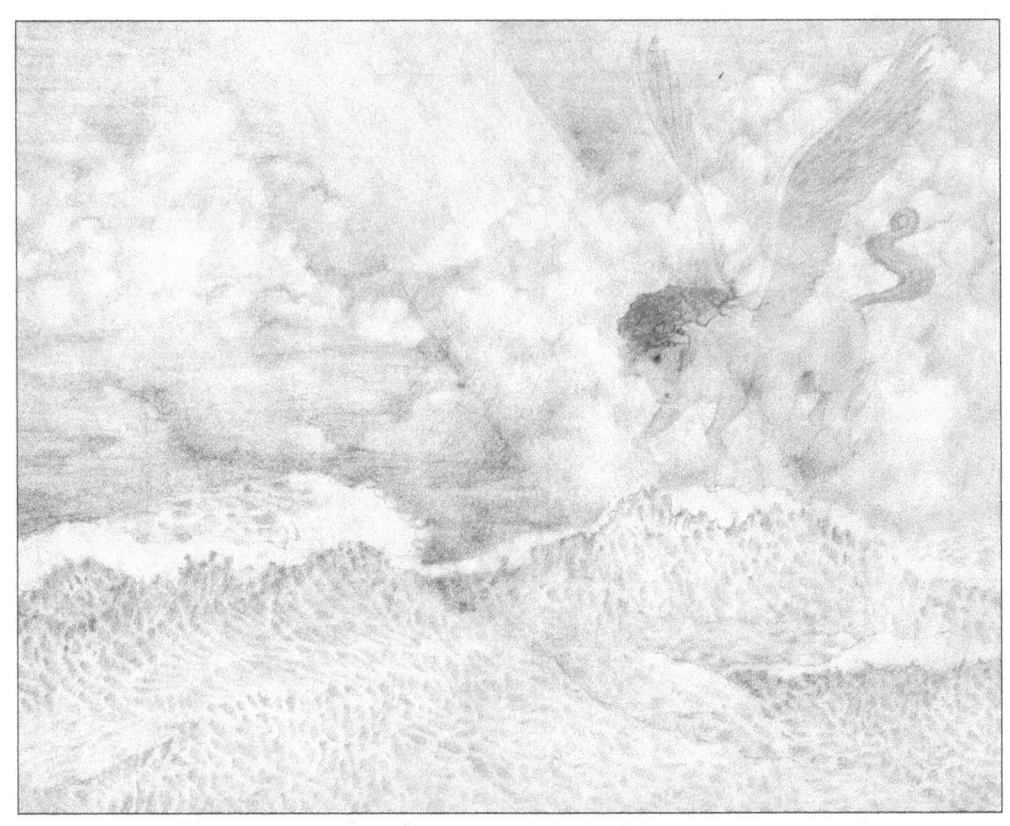

**But then appears a pegasus
"Do follow" does he say**

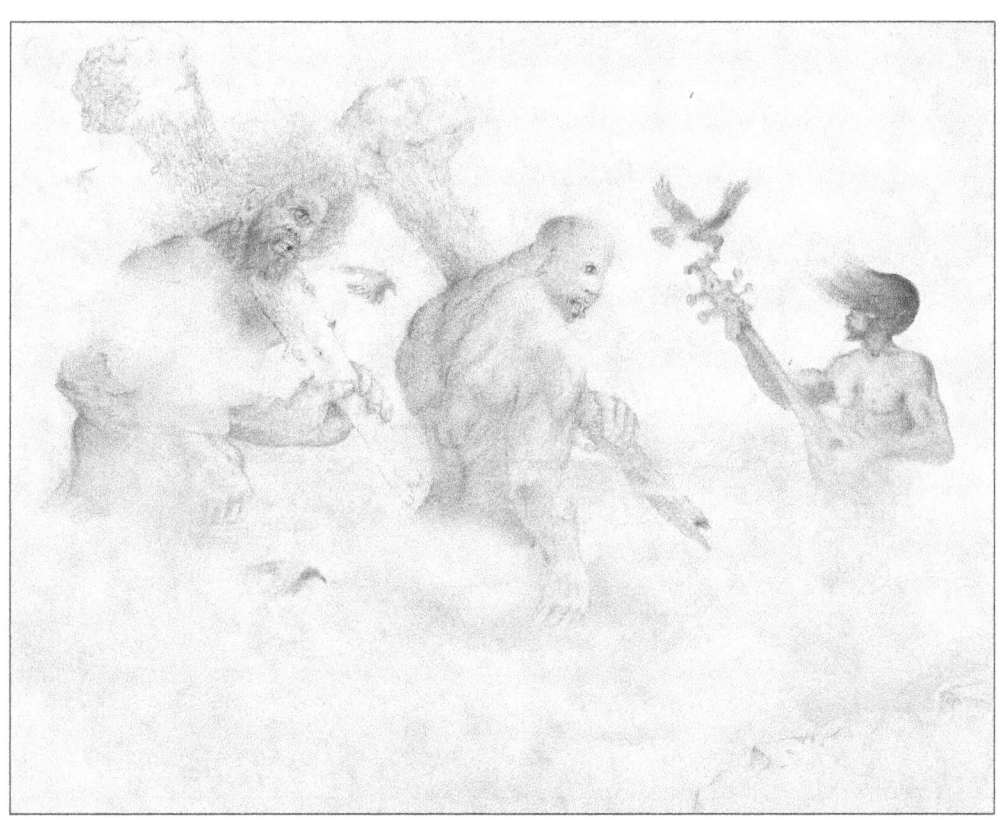

So to the isle of mythical beasts
The minstrel finds his way

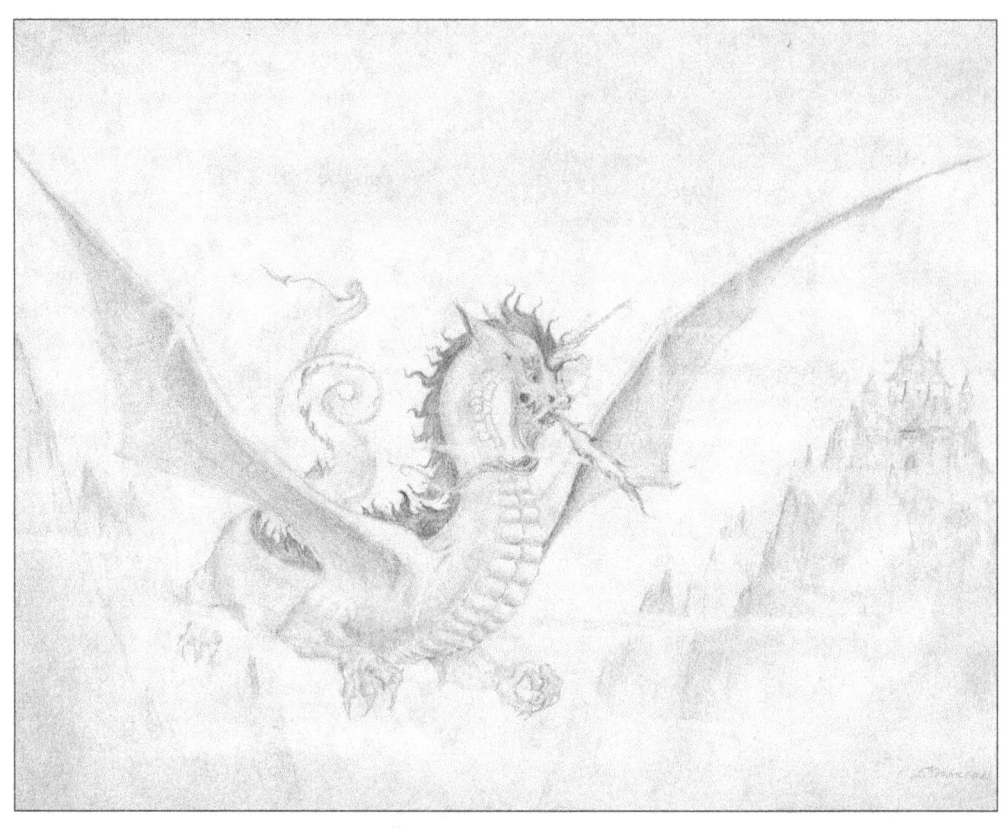

A dragon guards the forest
Where the unicorns reside
The minstrel must now come upon
A way to get inside

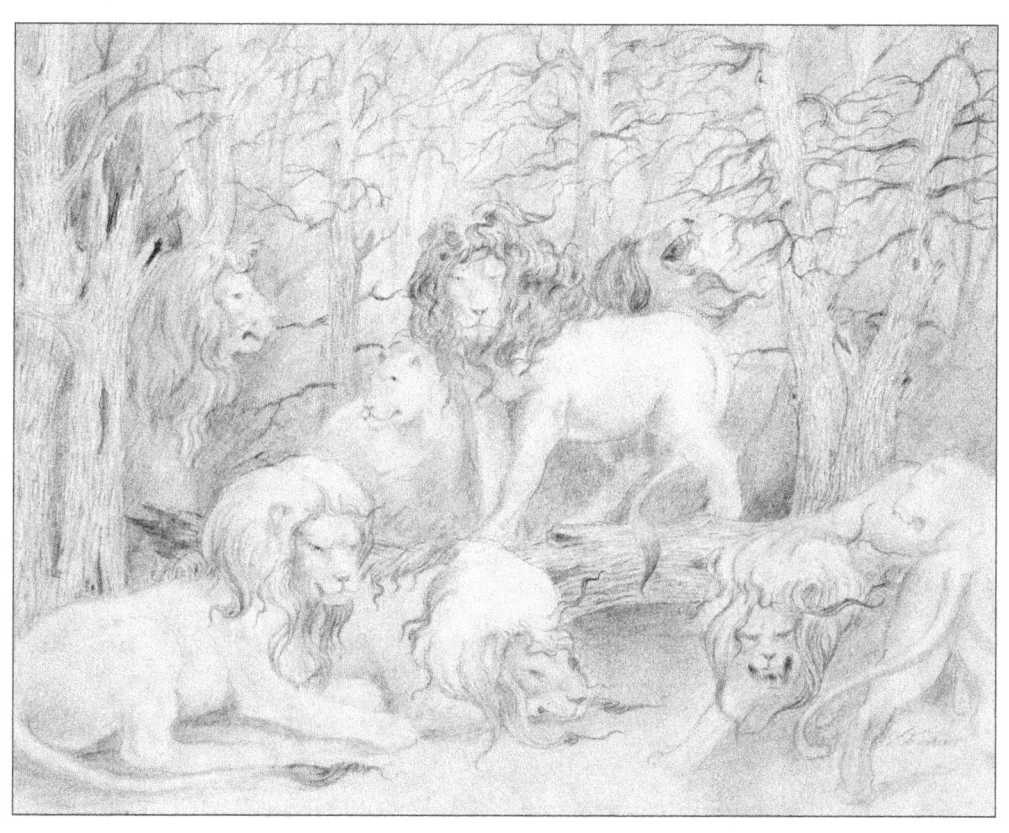

The lions pace about the edge
And growl to show their might
The minstrel sits and strums a tune
To calm the fearsome night

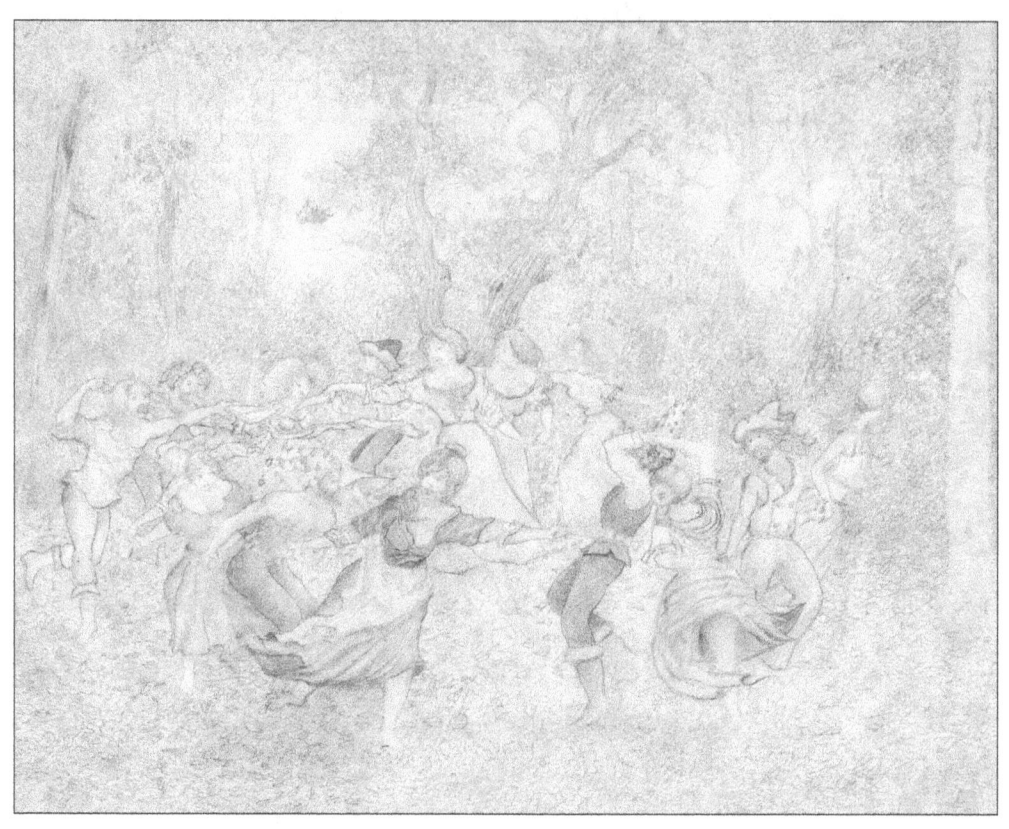

And when he opens up his eyes
The gypsies dance around

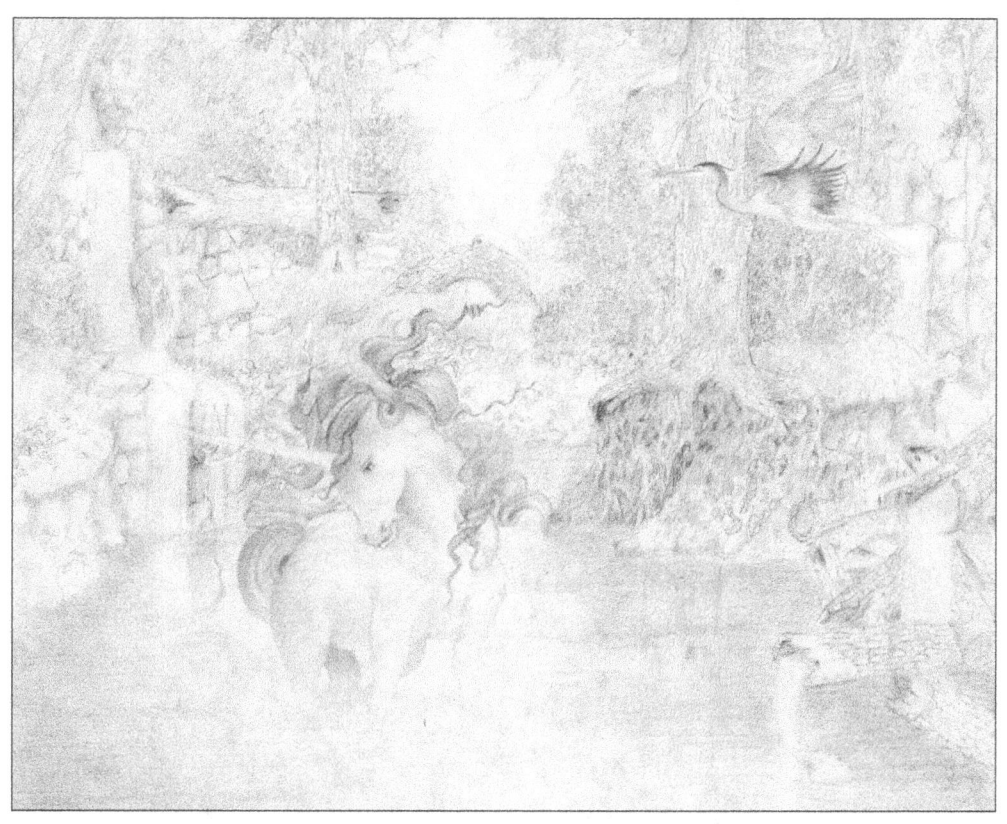

He follows them into the mist
The magic woods are found

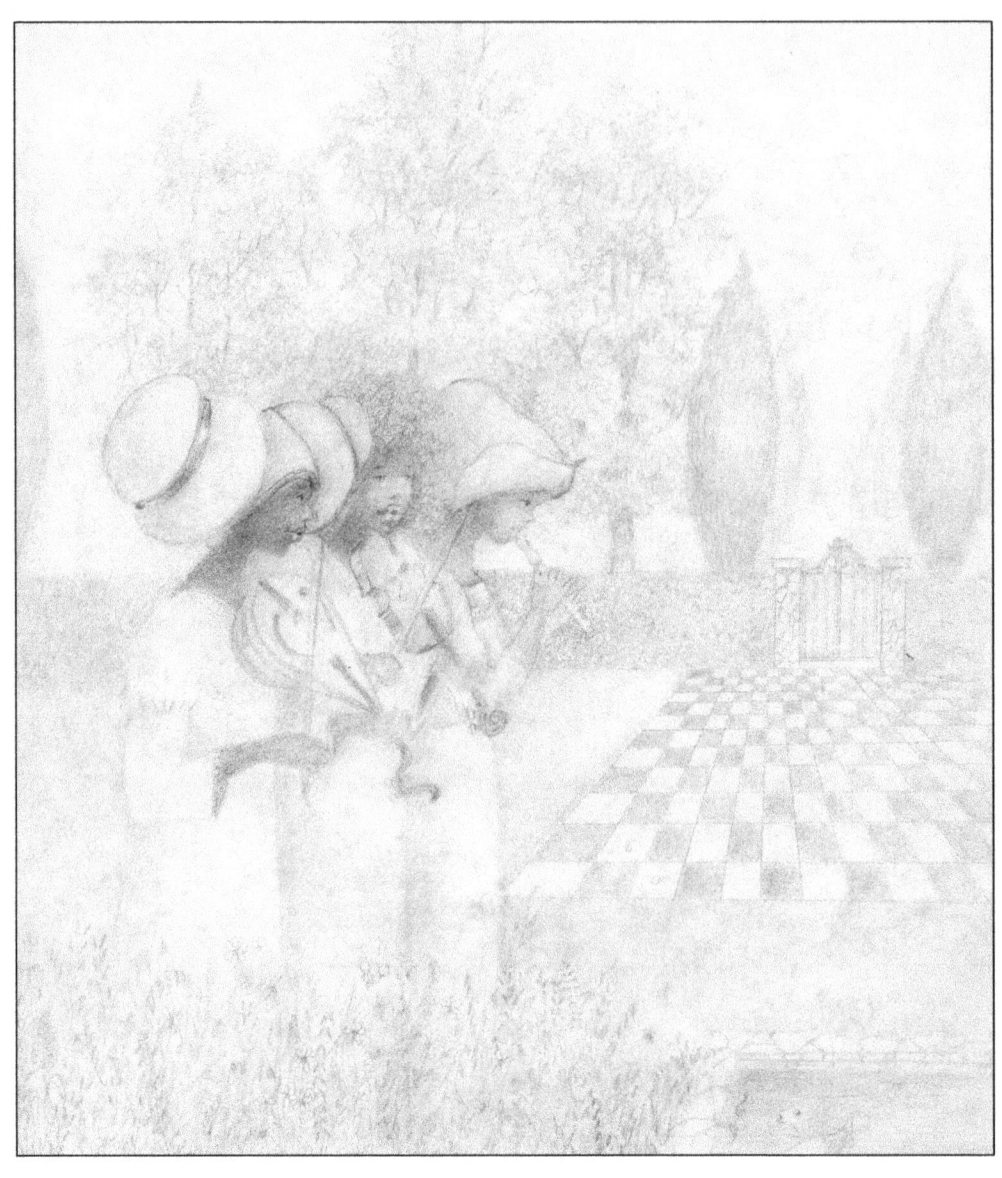

**At home the princess does lament
With music bittersweet**

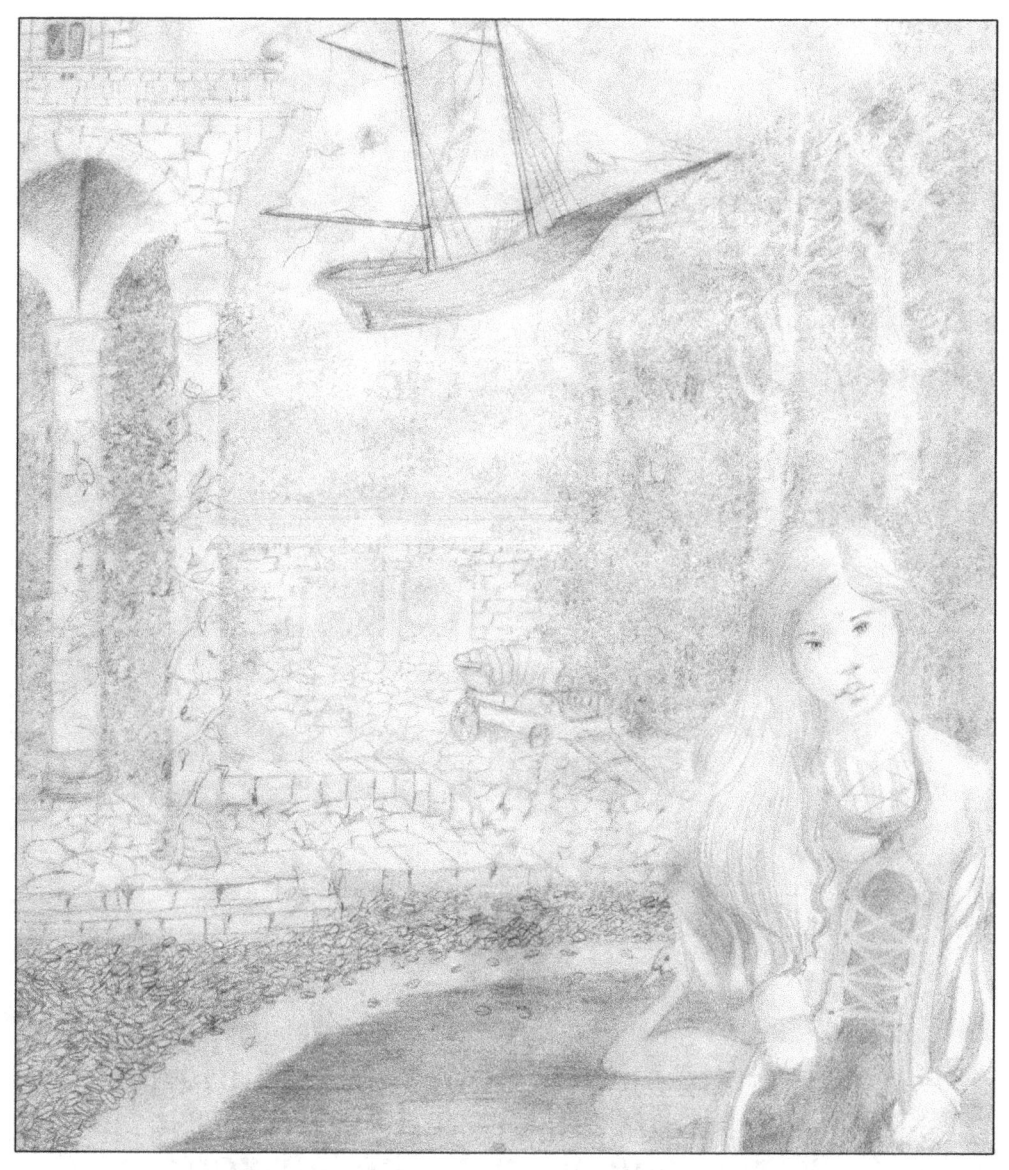

Long be the days since his farewell
Who knows when they shall meet

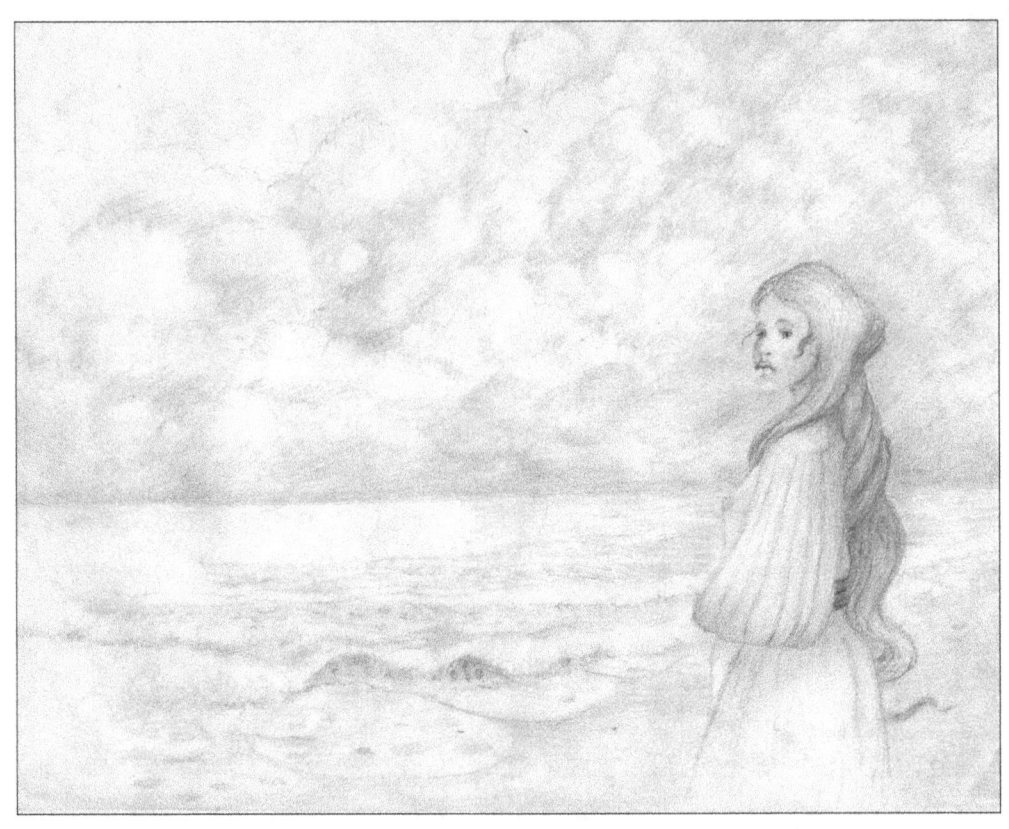

There she stands both day and night
Upon the ragged shore
Where she ponders the horizon
Will she wait forevermore

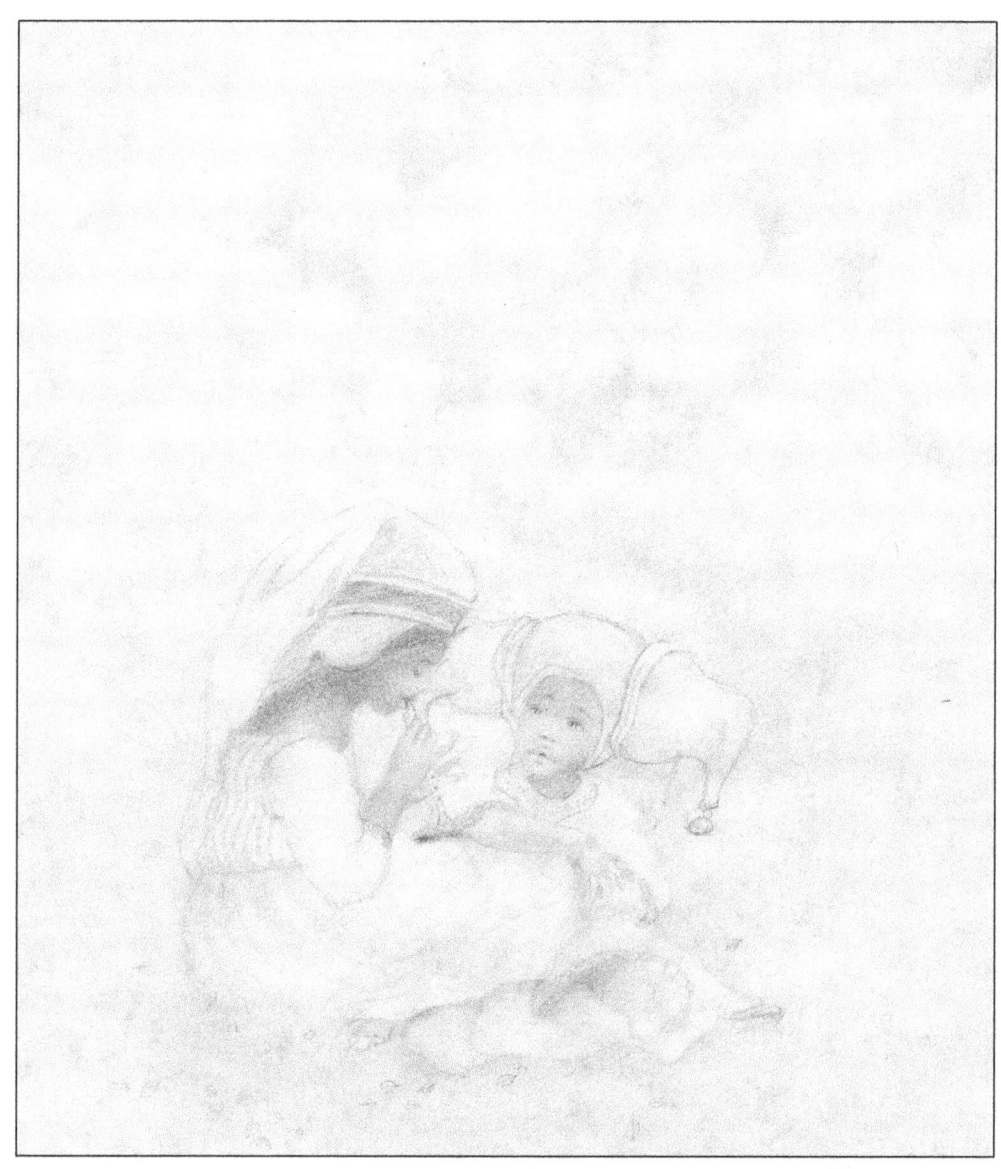

There's a gypsy in the courtyard
There are young girls by the fountain
While her love is chasing fairytales
On rainy purple mountain

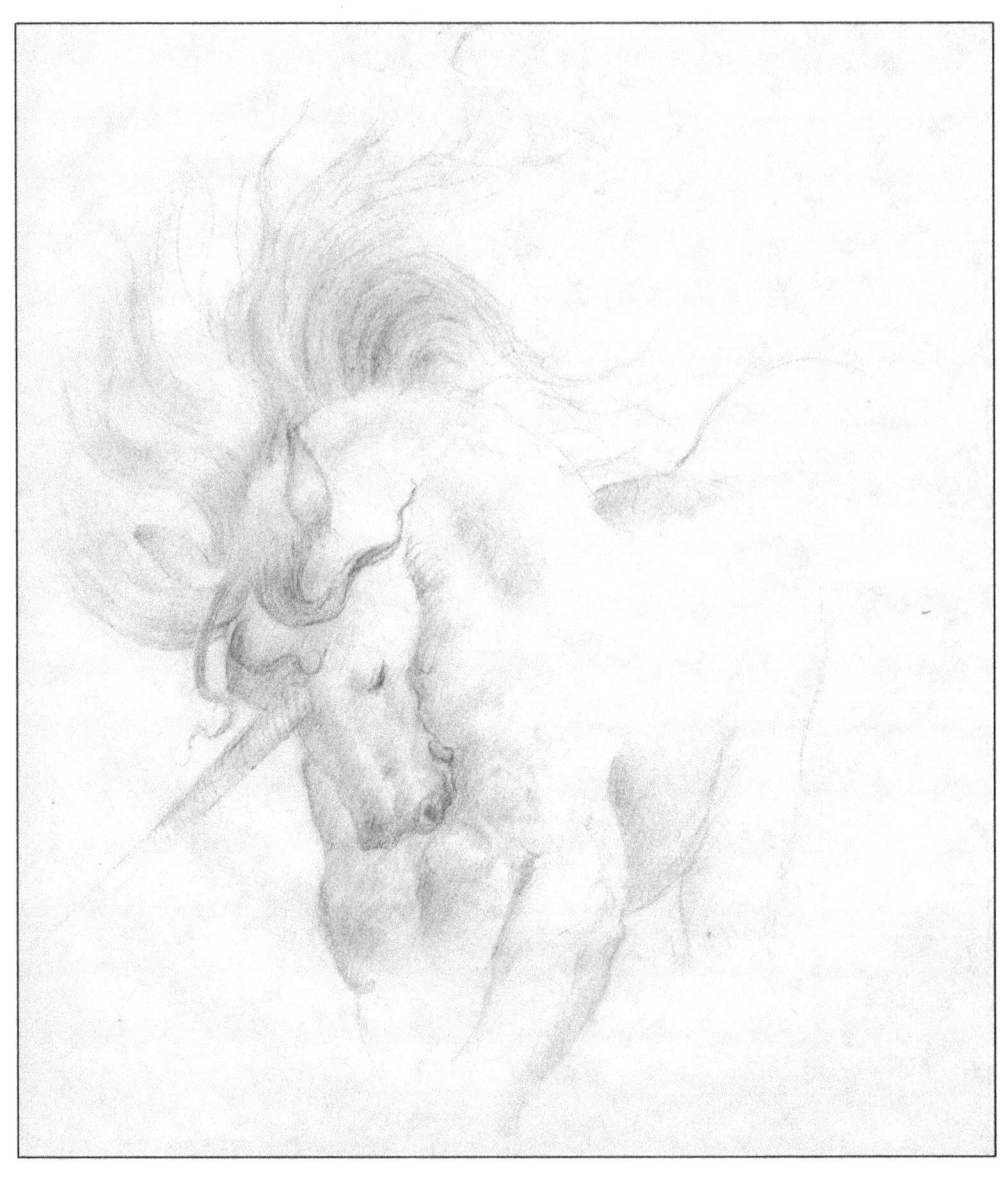

And there he finds the unicorns
So bright and fair and fast

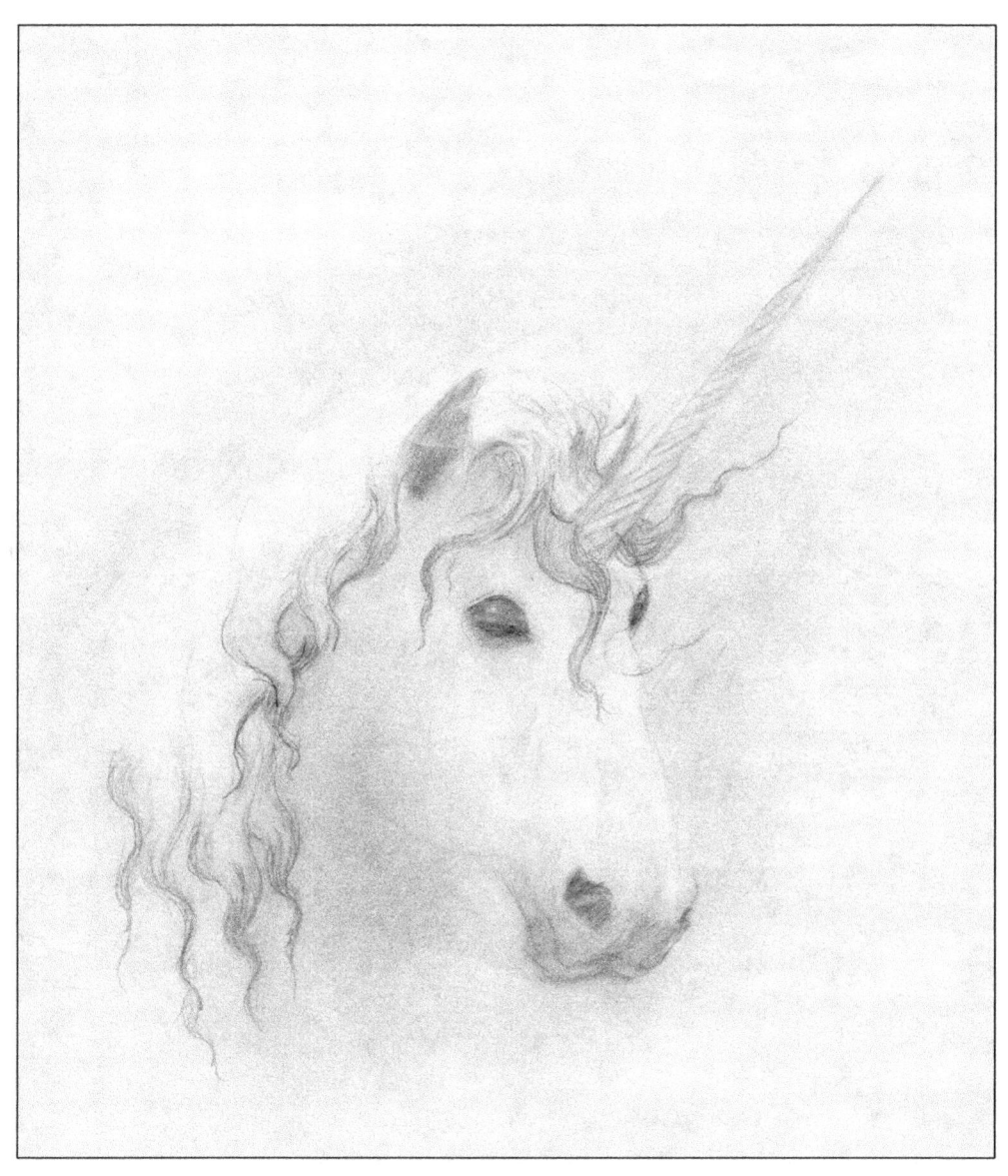

**Magnificent in all their light
His quest is won at last**

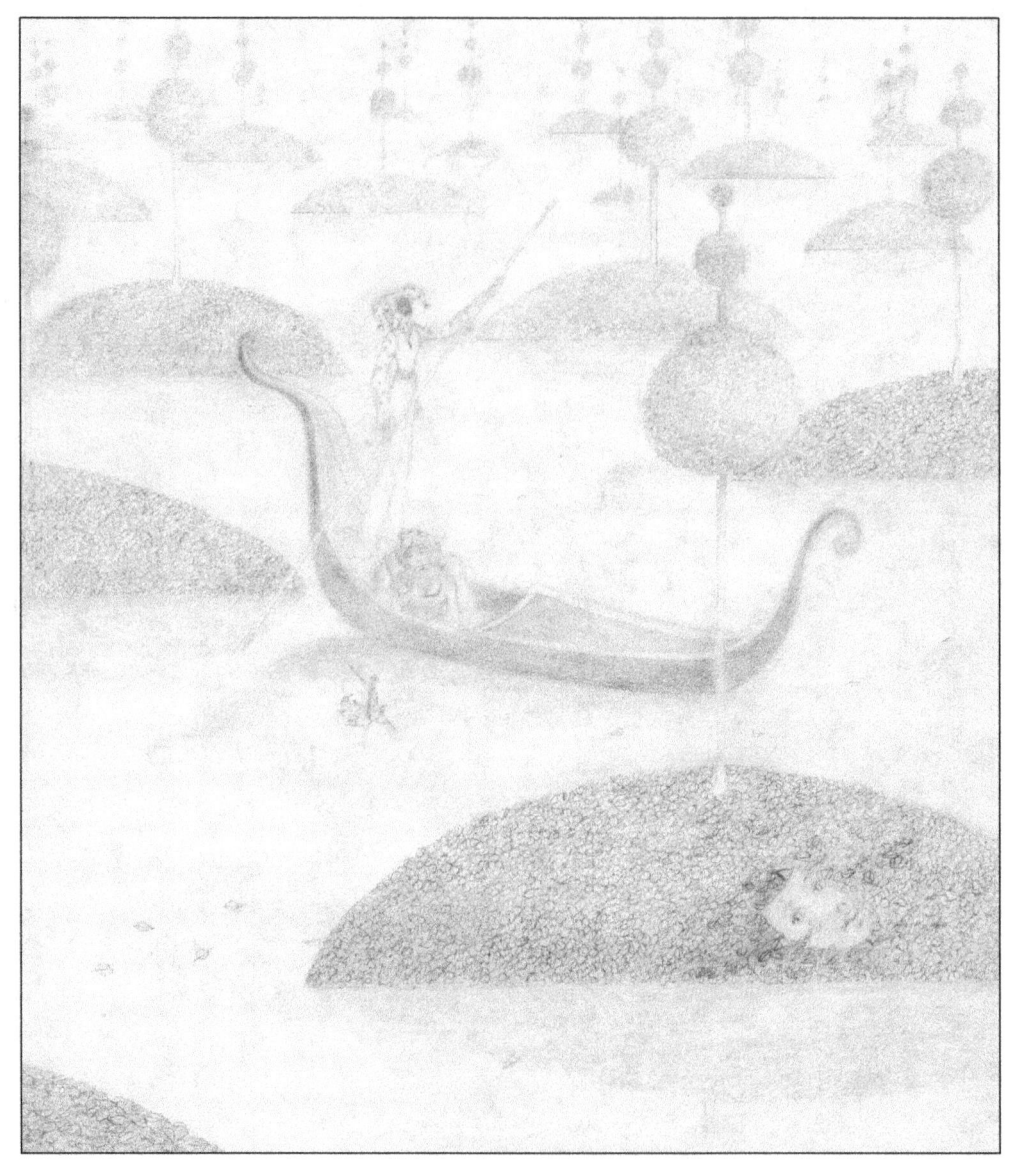

His love and he are gliding now
Upon a purple sea

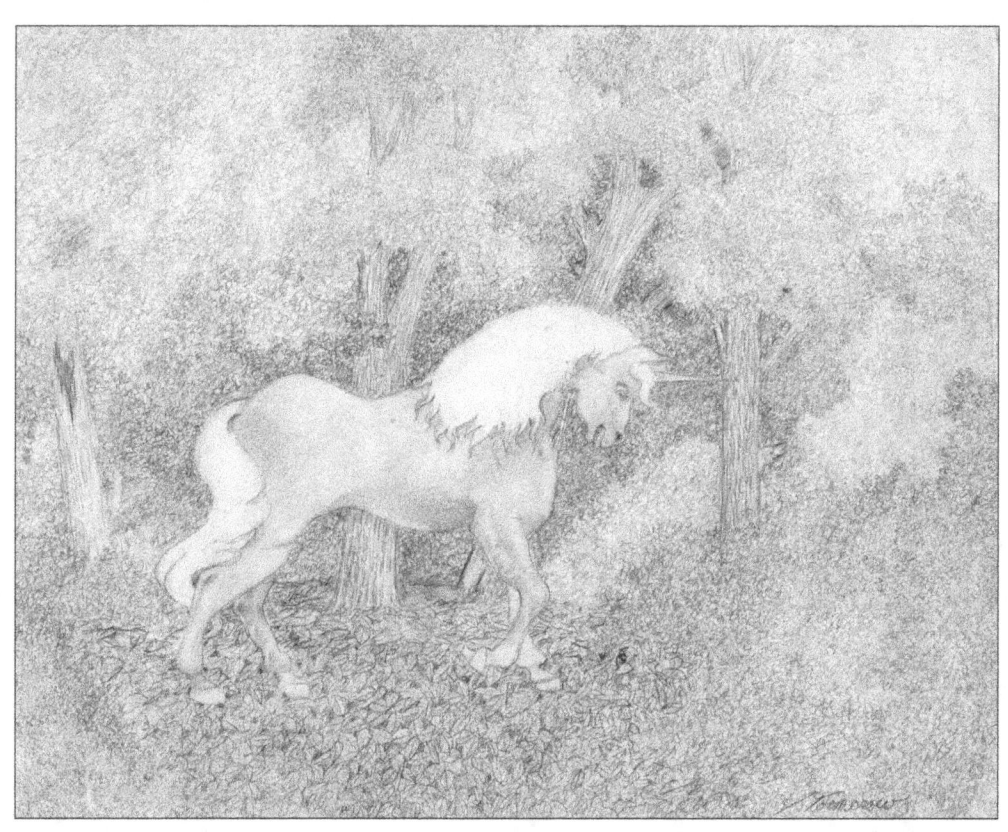

While unicorns they wander still
On isles of mystery

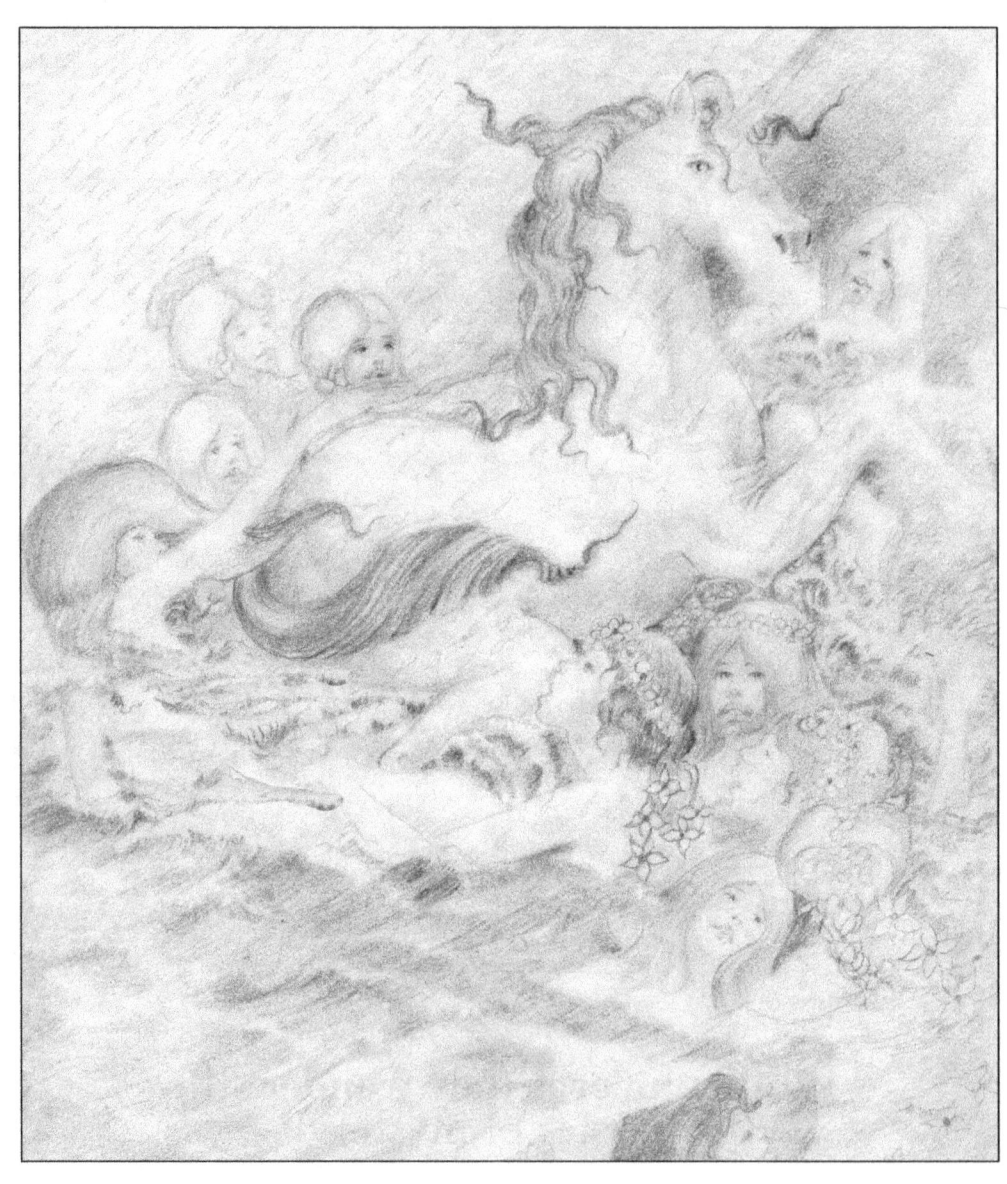

And so they live 'til end of years
In gentle reverie
Mysterious animals are we all
In life's menagerie

The End

The Moors

As a child growing up in Detroit, Michigan I had an aunt who was an artist. My father's sister, she used to tell us that our last name was Talifero because we were descended from the Moors (also knows as Muurs) of Venice. She used to tell us all kinds of tales about our ancestors. My father said it was just a bunch of fairytales and that we were descended from slaves like everyone else in our neighborhood.

She told of one ancestor who was a wandering minstrel and court jester who saved a King's son in battle and was made a Duke. He was given what was to be our ancestral lands and a certain amount of gold all of which was squandered within a year in sinister marketplaces.

My aunt Gloria totally believed the stories she would tell us. She was always doing research and showing my Father different documents that were supposed to prove the pedigree of our ancestry.

I loved her stories. It didn't really matter to me if they were true or not; just the possibility that we could be descended from the Moors of Venice set my mind to whirling. I would say that those stories had a definite outcome on the direction that my later life would take. Instead of playing basketball I studied art, learned to paint, fence, play chess, and handle a sailboat.

In my mid teens I did an intense amount of studying about the Moors. They came over from Africa and settled in Spain and Italy where they mingled with royalty. They brought with them our current numbering system which made it possible for the churches to build domes like Saint Peter's in Florence. They established one of the first libraries in Spain which soon became a center for scholars from all over the East as well as the West. They had a major influence on the architecture of the West.

The most famous Moor of course was Othello, a warrior who was very princely in his bearing. But there were many more who made major contributions to all of the arts. So when I wanted to choose a subject for an illustrated book I thought perhaps to cast a beam of light on this little known corner of Black history.

www.ingramcontent.com/pod-product-compliance
Lightning Source LLC
Chambersburg PA
CBHW081801170526
45167CB00008B/3275